DATE DUE

DEMCO 38-296

MOSCOW AND
THE MIDDLE EAST

MOSCOW AND THE MIDDLE EAST
NEW THINKING ON REGIONAL CONFLICT

Galia Golan

PUBLISHED IN NORTH AMERICA FOR

THE ROYAL INSTITUTE OF INTERNATIONAL AFFAIRS

COUNCIL ON FOREIGN RELATIONS PRESS
• NEW YORK •

Chatham House Papers

A Soviet Programme Publication
Programme Director: Neil Malcolm

The Royal Institute of International Affairs, at Chatham House in London, has provided an impartial forum for discussion and debate on current international issues for 70 years. Its resident research fellows, specialized information resources, and range of publications, conferences, and meetings span the fields of international politics, economics, and security. The Institute is independent of government.

Chatham House Papers are short monographs on current policy problems which have been commissioned by the RIIA. In preparing the papers, authors are advised by a study group of experts convened by the RIIA, and publication of a paper indicates that the Institute regards it as an authoritative contribution to the public debate. The Institute does not, however, hold opinions of its own; the views expressed in this publication are the responsibility of the author.

Library of Congress Cataloguing-in-Publication Data

Golan, Galia.
    Moscow and the Middle East : new thinking on regional conflict / Galia Golan.
        p. cm. -- (Chatham House paper)
    Originally published: London : Pinter Publishers, 1992
    Includes bibliographical references (p.   ).
    ISBN 0-87609-126-5 : $14.95
    1. Middle East--Foreign relations--Soviet Union. 2. Soviet Union--Foreign Relations--Middle East. 3. Israel-Arab conflicts. 4. Persian Gulf Region--Politics and government. I. Royal Institute of International Affairs. II. Title. III. Series: Chatham House papers (Unnumbered)
DS63.2.S65G645   1992
327.5694047--dc20
                                                        92-8545
                                                        CIP

92 93 94 95 96 97 PB 10 9 8 7 6 5 4 3 2 1

CONTENTS

ACKNOWLEDGMENTS

The staff of the Royal Institute of International Affairs, at Chatham House, have been extremely helpful in the preparation of this study. I am particularly indebted to Neil Malcolm for his penetrating and detailed comments on the manuscript at various stages. The discussion by members of the Chatham House study group was also invaluable, and I am grateful for the trouble so many people took to read and comment on the text. The opportunity to conduct research for this work was made possible by the accord between the RIIA and IMEMO, the Institute of World Economy and International Relations of the Academy of Sciences in Moscow. The research in the Soviet Union was extremely worthwhile, and I should like to thank IMEMO, and especially Nodari Simoniya, Vladimir Nosenko, and Vladimir Rybakov, as well as experts from other institutes (the Institute for the Study of the USA and Canada, the Oriental Institute, the Africa Institute), the Foreign Ministry, the Russian Parliament and the press for their time and insights. In Jerusalem I am indebted to the Mayrock Centre for Soviet and East European Research of the Hebrew University and to my research assistant, Mark Assaraf.

Jerusalem, January 1992   Galia Golan

1
INTRODUCTION

This study, originally conceived as an assessment of current Soviet policies, has not proved easy to complete. In the course of its preparation the Soviet Union has ceased to exist as a political entity, and its replacement, the Commonwealth of Independent States, remains only in the early stages of formation. Indeed, as we go to press, the book is on the verge of becoming a historical analysis rather than a study of current policy. With the resignation of Mikhail Gorbachev and the dissolution of the Soviet Union, a dividing line may now be drawn between Soviet policy under Gorbachev on the one side, and, on the other side, the policies of Russia, Ukraine, the Central Asian Republics, indeed some fifteen new states, and/or the new Commonwealth binding (possibly) most but not all of the former Soviet republics.

This does not, however, detract from the momentousness of the changes that took place between 1985 and 1991. Under Gorbachev the Soviet Union evolved a consistent, purposeful policy in the Middle East. The Soviet approach to the region gradually underwent an almost total transformation in keeping with the 'new political thinking', the foreign policy component of perestroika. New thinking has had a monumental impact on the region, as on the whole world, not least because of the unprecedented Soviet–American cooperation and the willingness of the

1

parties concerned to seek a peace agreement in the Arab–Israeli conflict. We shall, therefore, examine the principles of new thinking, particularly those most relevant to policy in the region, in Chapter 2. This will be followed by a chapter assessing the most complex and perhaps the central application of the theory: the Arab–Israeli conflict. A second range of issues will be dealt with in Chapter 4, which examines the application of Gorbachev's policies to the Persian Gulf area. The crucial test of new thinking in all its aspects came, however, with the Gulf crisis and war in 1990–1. The ramifications of Gorbachev's often inconsistent policies throughout this crisis to a large degree confirmed as well as consolidated the groundwork laid by the application of new thinking to both the Arab–Israeli conflict and the Gulf states; these ramifications will be treated in Chapter 5. An epilogue examines some of the issues and questions raised with regard to possible future policies as a result of the break-up of the Union in the aftermath of the attempted coup in August 1991.

2
NEW THINKING IN SOVIET FOREIGN POLICY

The 'new thinking' on which Gorbachev's Middle East policy was based was born of a number of very practical considerations, not least of which were the prohibitive economic costs of the Soviet Union's competition with the West and the need for a respite from international tensions so as to facilitate and concentrate upon the resolution of domestic, particularly economic, problems. In its practical aspects, therefore, new thinking might be viewed as no different from Leonid Brezhnev's earlier policy of detente, interpreted in the most negative cold-war terms as the achievement of a comfortable – and safe – international environment so as to bolster the Soviet economy and interests abroad in the continued competition with the West.

Yet new thinking was also born of an altogether new conceptualization of Soviet foreign policy and a different view of the place and role of the Soviet Union in the world today. One might argue, as I do not, that this new conceptualization itself was born of purely practical considerations or, more cynically, that it was no more than a hollow rationalization for what was merely a new tactic designed to achieve the same old goals of Soviet expansionism and eventual world domination. Whatever his original intentions, however, Gorbachev and his advisers soon gave new thinking both content and strategic significance, producing, in fact, an entirely new foreign policy for the Soviet Union. This applied in time to the Middle East as well as to the United States, Europe and the West in general.

In its broadest terms, new thinking posited the idea of global inter-dependence, generated by the existence of a world economy and the universal nature of such problems as nuclear conflict, the environment, natural resources and international terrorism. The interdependence created by the modern era dictated, according to new thinking, a 'de-ideo-logization' of foreign policy and the search for a balance of interests between states rather than the pursuit of zero-sum-game competition. New thinking eschewed competition, not only perhaps because of a belief that the Soviet Union could not win, but out of a conviction that it did not need to win. By positing an interdependent world and the removal of ideology, Gorbachev eliminated the rationale and potential for the zero-sum-game approach. In so doing he also provided the basis for a new attitude to the Third World and a different role for the Soviet armed forces, emanating from a new military doctrine. All of this combined to produce a new view of regional conflict.

Attitude to the Third World and regional conflict

A renunciation of ideology with regard to the Third World was based in part on an admission that Moscow had failed in its attempt to provide a compelling model of development as an alternative to the capitalist West. Abandoning the competition altogether, Soviet policy towards the Third World was to be guided by the need for a balance of interests and the priority of Soviet national, i.e. domestic, interests. Relations could thus be maintained with states of various socio-economic systems on a prag-matic basis, with neither the need nor the justification for power projec-tion on the part of the Soviet armed forces. This reflected the military doctrine dictated by new thinking – that is, the doctrine of reasonable defensive sufficiency, in which the power projection or 'external func-tion' of the Soviet armed forces, along with the idea of nuclear deter-rence, were to be replaced by a doctrine limited to the defence of the Soviet Union.[1]

The new doctrine would thus take the Soviet armed forces out of regional conflicts. The Clausewitzian approach (war as a continuation of politics by other means), formerly espoused by Lenin, was explicitly rejected in the demand for reliance solely upon political solutions to conflict. In an interdependent world, attempts at military solutions, or even the existence of regional conflicts, threatened global security.[2] This was not a new concern in Soviet military doctrine; the new element was the Soviet Union's admission that its own involvement in regional conflicts might impede progress at the superpower level, as it had done in the past.[3] Thus Brezhnev's old 'divisibility of detente' (which allowed for one policy at the superpower level and another at the regional) was explicitly discarded. Such concrete factors as the effects of regional developments on the maintenance of arms agreements between the United States and the Soviet Union were now seriously to be considered.[4]

Beyond the purely military aspects, foreign policy thinkers in Moscow, including the leadership, advocated the removal of the superpowers from regional conflict altogether. If this were done, regional conflicts would be greatly restricted in scope and danger, and their persistence possibly checked. For without the superpowers' aid and encouragement, the parties involved would find it increasingly difficult to pursue conflict. Moreover, withdrawal of the superpowers would reduce conflicts to their local – presumably more easily handled – causes, making them subject to resolution on the basis of a balance of interests or of 'national reconciliation', depending on the type of conflict involved. The end of the zero-sum-game East–West competition rendered such a withdrawal possible, removing also the power of the local actors to exploit that competition in their pursuit of conflict. The superpowers might assist in the resolution of the conflict, but they could no longer be pitted against each other in order to perpetuate it.[5]

The superpowers' role, then, would be a collective or at least a cooperative one, although new thinking placed greater emphasis on multilateral collective efforts, that is, on international bodies such as the United Nations or World Court. In theory this reflected the interdependent nature of the international system and coincided with the advocated shift to abiding by international laws and norms of behaviour. More pragmatically, the reliance upon collective bodies may have been intended as a device to overcome or obfuscate the asymmetry of the superpowers' actual power and position in the world – in which the Soviet Union was very much secondary to the United States.

Contradictions and dilemmas

There were contradictions, or at least dilemmas, in the new approach. And to a certain degree the Soviets themselves were willing to acknowledge some of them. First and most obvious was the contradiction between withdrawal from regional conflict and the maintenance nonetheless of the Soviet Union's status as a great power. Both popular opinion and elite attitudes, according to a study of Soviet foreign policy elites conducted in 1989, strongly favoured withdrawal and a reduction of Soviet involvement in Third World endeavours.[6] Yet they also strongly opposed loss of the country's prestige and great-power status in the world. Concern over the resultant decline in Soviet status, if not in actual power, could be found particularly among Communist Party officials, Russian nationalists and the military, although the aspiration to great-power status was a traditional one, shared, even if only passively, by a large portion of the general public.

Second, there was the more concrete problem of seeking political solutions and disengaging so as to reduce the military potential of conflicts when, in fact, the Soviet economy was in need of the hard-currency earnings deriving from arms sales generated by such conflicts. Soviet officials increasingly admitted this second problem, proposing that it be discussed in the Supreme Soviet as well as in public debate.[7] New thinkers opposed to such sales on moral as well as political or theoretical grounds argued that there was in fact not even any economic basis to these sales, since most buyers outside the Warsaw Pact were Third World nations unable to meet the hard-currency payments owed for the arms. It was pointed out that even Libya still owed the Soviet Union $2 billion; some claimed such 'sales' had been one great foreign aid programme.[8] Indeed the total debt to the Soviet Union has been estimated at between $90 and $130 billion.

These claims were countered by military officials, one of whom argued that arms sales constituted 15% of Soviet hard-currency earnings and were therefore economically essential.[9] A related argument actually focused on the absence of official figures as to just how worthwhile or large the arms business was for the Soviet Union. Indeed a Soviet admiral, Deputy Minister for Foreign Economic Relations, responded to an interviewer's question on this with the comment that revelation of the figures would be too dangerous politically, causing an 'information bomb'.[10] Thus, to the argument that the military should be subordinated to domestic concerns in the determination of Soviet foreign policy, the military could and did respond with the economic argument. This not only had the obvious support of the powerful military industries but indirectly bolstered various groups interested in the maintenance of Soviet involvement overseas for reasons of status and military-political power.

The impact of domestic problems

The main focus of new thinking was neither the Third World nor regional conflict, but rather superpower relations and relations with the West. Moreover, the scale of Soviet domestic problems rendered foreign policy and military doctrine – whatever their thrust – far less central issues for discussion or concern. The crumbling Soviet federation and deteriorating economy, coupled with a breakdown in law and order, political instability and ethnic strife, combined to dwarf if not eliminate the almost theoretical questions of overseas involvement or superpower competition in far-flung regions of the world.

Yet domestic and foreign policy questions were intimately related, as the already noted contradictions have indicated. There were powerful political forces that sought to use foreign policy issues, even if only symbolically, in their domestic struggle for and against perestroika. In the pluralistic society that was developing, interest groups – whether Russian nationalists, Muslims, Jews or others – in addition to such power-bases as the military, the KGB and the Party, perceived certain aspects of foreign policy as part and parcel of their own interests. Thus not only did the issue of arms sales strengthen the hand of conservative military elements but such factors and events as the independence of Eastern Europe and the break-up of the Warsaw Pact, the conventional arms agreement in Europe, the reunification of Germany and the war against Iraq all had a further impact on the domestic political struggle, threatening perestroika altogether by 1990–1. Moreover, regional issues and conflicts directly involved the Soviet Union with the West, in some cases threatening the nascent superpower relationship, and thereby in turn threatening the assistance and Western cooperation that were essential to the pursuit of perestroika at home.

Institutional changes

New thinking also dictated institutional changes in the foreign policy establishment of the Soviet Union. If domestic considerations were to determine the national interest, popular opinion was to play a greater role in the formulation of foreign policy. In keeping with the democratization component of perestroika, channels for the expression and transmission of popular sentiment were to be devised while the dictatorship of the Party in these (as well as other) affairs was to be ended. As a result, foreign policy decision-making was to shift to the Foreign Ministry (from the Party's International Department, Secretariat and Politburo), a critical role being allocated to the International Affairs Committee of the Supreme Soviet. Just where military decision-making was to be concentrated was not entirely clear, although in theory the military was also to be subject to parliamentary control; decisions were to rest ultimately with the Defence Council of the government, headed by President Gorbachev.

Although the Foreign Ministry did in fact assume a greater role at the expense of the Party, it was the President and his advisers (a personal cabinet that went through a number of incarnations, including the Presidential Council and later the National Security Council) who became the main decision-makers. The authority and jurisdiction of these advisers (led by the principal architect of new thinking, Aleksandr Yakovlev) and these Councils (which comprised the chief government ministers as well as some of the advisers, such as Evgeny Primakov) remained obscure. While the Party struggled to regain its power over the government ministries, there was little clarity as to the authority of these newly strengthened ministries themselves. It was not clear, for example, just where Defence Ministry jurisdiction stopped and Foreign Ministry jurisdiction began with regard to such crucial questions as arms sales or the dispatch of military advisers abroad. Moreover, the parliamentary committees designed to supervise and control decisions on such matters tended to be dominated, numerically, by the very officials (military and other) whose interests were involved – which greatly reduced the committees' efficacy as controlling bodies.

At the same time, the growing strength of the various Soviet republics gave birth to still other foreign policy bodies: the foreign ministries of these republics and the international affairs committees of their parliaments. Of enormous potential if not actual importance was the role that might be played by the International Affairs Committee of the Supreme Soviet of the Russian Republic (RSFSR), headed by the highly competent and respected new thinker, Vladimir Lukin, or by the RSFSR's Foreign Minister, Andrei Kozyrev, as adviser to Russian President Boris Yeltsin. The emergence of the republics in foreign affairs carried with it serious implications for the delineation and conduct of a unified Soviet foreign policy, posing complex constitutional questions that arose particularly in the event of disagreement between the two levels. Ambiguity in the decision-making process, institutional changes and the nationalities issue, in addition to the domestic political struggle, the new military doctrine and approach to the Third World (including regional conflict) generated by the new conceptualization of foreign policy without Marxist-Leninist ideology – all these, combined, were to have an inevitable impact on Soviet policy in the Middle East, as well as everywhere else.

3

THE ARAB–ISRAELI CONFLICT

Application of new thinking to the Middle East

New thinking, with all the attributes and dilemmas outlined in Chapter 2, was applied to the Arab–Israeli conflict as well as to other regional conflicts.[1] This could be seen in the Soviet attitude to the conflict itself, to the parties involved, to the type of settlement sought and to the means for bringing about a settlement. If the zero-sum game were obsolete, and ideology removed from foreign policy, then the Arab–Israeli conflict, like many others, would lose much of its appeal for the Soviet Union. It had already been losing its value as a vehicle for Soviet competition with the West, or at least as a productive vehicle.[2] With the end of the competition, there was little political or strategic gain to be sought. What remained of Soviet interests in the region might be obtainable without the conflict, for these were defensive interests more directly associated with the northern tier of Middle Eastern states bordering on the Soviet Union. Under a doctrine of defensive sufficiency rather than power projection, protection of the Soviet Union's southern border, including safeguarding it against the disruptive spread of Islamic fundamentalism among the restive Muslim ethnic groups of Central Asia, would gain ascendancy.

The other primary interest in the region was economic, with the greatest potential from the Soviet point of view emanating from the oil-rich Gulf states. Aside from revenues from arms sales, the Soviet

Union had an interest in expanded trade, credits and joint or tripartite ventures with these states (and Israel). These interests would not only remain if the Arab–Israeli conflict were resolved, they might even be more easily and successfully pursued in conditions of stability. Withdrawal from direct involvement and commitment to their respective clients might reduce the risks of confrontation between the superpowers. Yet the continued threat of war and periodic tensions generated by the Arab–Israeli conflict could produce strains on the superpower relationship, challenging and possibly crippling any attempt to remain aloof. Moreover, the ongoing conflict produced risks of another kind and serious pressures on Moscow (as well as on Washington). The arms race in the region was taking an alarming turn in the direction of non-conventional weapons and the development of systems which could threaten states beyond the region. The presence of intermediate-range missiles, the development of anti-ballistic missile (ABM) capabilities, and the spread of nuclear, chemical and biological warfare potential could place the efficacy of the superpowers' arms agreements in doubt.[3]

The Soviet response to the arms race – namely, willingness to continue to supply ever more advanced weapons including aircraft to Syria, for example – became something of a litmus test for perestroika/new thinking in the eyes of the United States. At the very least it became an excuse (although not the main one) for increased American arms sales to the region. Yet significant cutbacks in the supply of arms – particularly the limitation of supplies to what Moscow considered 'reasonable defensive sufficiency' rather than the 'strategic parity' demanded by Damascus, for example, in time of continuing conflict with Israel – created strains in Soviet-Arab relations.[4] In fact this was but one source of the strained relationship with the Arabs that was producing pressures on the Soviet leadership, as we shall see below.[5] Unlike in the past, however, Moscow could not eliminate these pressures through a position similar to 'divisibility of detente'. Moreover, despite the fact that the end of the zero-sum approach obviated the need to oblige its clients for fear of their bolting to the Americans, Moscow was reluctant to ignore them and completely abandon its influence. This unwillingness was generated not only by Soviet economic or border-related interests in the region but also by the dilemma already mentioned: the urge, if not for empire, then at least for maintenance of great-power status.

Domestic pressures

There were also a number of domestic reasons why Moscow could not simply ignore Arab pressures.

The pro-Arab lobby

In the new circumstances within the Soviet Union there was something of a 'pro-Arab lobby'.[6] These were people who argued for loyalty to Moscow's past allies and friends in Soviet Middle East policy; they opposed steps that might weaken the Arabs and/or benefit Israel. Those associated with this position appeared to be the 'Arabists' – whether within the Party, the Foreign Ministry, the research institutes or the press. For example, a top Middle East expert of the Party's International Department, Yury Griadunov, who was transferred to Jordan as Soviet ambassador in 1990, may have been one such person.[7] While his section, like the International Department itself, was greatly reduced as a result of perestroika, Party positions regarding this area may have been greatly influenced by Aleksandr Dzasokhov, a Politburo member (responsible for ideology), former ambassador to Syria and former head of the Soviet Afro-Asian Solidarity Committee. He was both an old Middle East hand and a conservative who also served as head of the International Affairs Committee of the Supreme Soviet. Vladimir Polyakov, head of the Middle East Department of the Foreign Ministry until he was sent to Egypt as ambassador in 1990, had spoken out in favour of loyalty to Moscow's Arab friends. His replacement, Vasily Kolotusha, the Soviet ambassador to Lebanon, was rumoured to hold similar views.[8] Generally of the same type was Vitaly Naumkin, one of the leading researchers and a consultant on Middle Eastern affairs; he was in charge of this region at the Academy of Sciences' Oriental Institute, which was under the conservative leadership of Mikhail Kapitsa.[9] And journalists such as Karen Geivandov and Igor Belyaev, old Middle East hands, together with Novosti's Aleksandr Smirnov (deputy head of the Middle East section) were slow to abandon their defence of Arab claims, including even occasional support for Palestinian terrorist acts.[10] Somewhat more open but tending still in this direction were *Pravda*'s Middle East specialist Yury Glukhov and the deputy director of the Africa Institute, former *Pravda* correspondent Aleksei Vasiliev.

The Muslim factor

Some force may have been given to their arguments by Soviet Muslims, whose voice was of obvious importance not only by virtue of their numbers (over 45 million) but also because of their disruptive nationalism, particularly in Soviet republics bordering the Middle East. Soviet Muslim republics became actively involved in religious and business contacts with Muslim states such as Iran, Pakistan, Saudi Arabia and the Gulf states. Saudi Arabia, for example, established a bank in Kazakhstan, and Kuwait provided funds for a Muslim university there.[11] That these contacts could have clear foreign policy implications was demonstrated not only by the expressed wish of some, like the Tartar President, to have direct diplomatic relations with Muslim countries, but also, at the popular level, by the many requests from Soviet Muslims to volunteer to fight for Saddam Hussein during the Gulf crisis. A slogan in evidence at the opening of a centre for Islam in Moscow in June 1991 called for the 'liberation of Jerusalem and occupied Palestine'. Some 800,000 Muslims, including 300,000 Tartars, resided in Moscow. While the Muslim population still did not constitute a majority in the Soviet Union or in the Russian Republic, many Russians, at any rate, were inclined to view this element with a degree of concern in the realm of foreign policy as well as domestic decisions. Some tended to exaggerate this, and conservative Arabists were able to use it as a pretext to justify their less friendly attitudes towards Israel.

In fact, foreign policy was not high on the agenda of complaints and demands of Soviet Muslims. Moreover, the majority of Soviet Muslims were of Turkic origin and defined their national identity not only in Muslim terms but in terms of Turkish culture. For the most part Sunni rather than Shi'a, their revived attraction to Islam was linked more with nationalist sentiments than with fundamentalism of the Iranian type, except in the case of Tadjikistan or, possibly, of young people throughout the Central Asian republics. Nonetheless, the Soviet 'Muslim factor' was at least potentially important for the determination of policy towards the Arab–Israeli conflict or the region in general.[12]

Nationalism and anti-Semitism

Greater influence of a more immediate nature was attributable to Russian nationalists with anti-Semitic tendencies, often of a virulent type such as

13

the anti-Semitism of the extremist group Pamyat'. Their sentiments extended to an anti-Zionism similar to that expressed by the Public Committee Against Zionism and the Public Committee Against Resumption of Diplomatic Relations with Israel. The net effect of their basically negative approach was to promote Arab interests; indeed their arguments often took the form of championing the Arabs against 'Jewish racism'.[13] Domestically they were associated with the conservative, anti-perestroika camp, as positions on the Arab–Israeli conflict came, in some circles, symbolically to connote domestic political positions. Thus their voices augmented those concerned with the maintenance of the Soviet Union's position as a great power in the world and those more pragmatically anxious about economic losses from cutbacks in arms sales, as well as those identifiable as military discontents.

Military discontent

It was in fact these last elements which constituted the strongest pressure groups favouring maintenance of pre-Gorbachev positions in the Middle East. The Defence Ministry, particularly those connected with the military industries inside and outside the Ministry, as well as high-level military personnel, were strong lobbyists for the preservation of Soviet interests – and positions – in the Arab world. For many of them, this was part and parcel of their general dissatisfaction with perestroika and new thinking, policies which had led to such events as the virtual break-up of the Warsaw Pact and arms agreements that they perceived as having seriously weakened the Soviet Union in military terms, to the benefit of the United States.[14] Thus theirs was a position which often merged with the anti-perestroika agitation of the conservative, mainly Communist Party, group in the Soviet parliament, Soyuz, with spokespersons such as Colonel Viktor Alksnis.

Pro-perestroika pressures

Facing these groups were the proponents of the application of new thinking to the Middle East. Some of them formed the Public Committee for Renewal of Diplomatic Relations with Israel. This committee, composed of many non-Jews as well as Jews, sought to counter the anti-Zionists and anti-Semites. Just as these last were identified with an anti-perestroika position, so the proponents of renewed relations could be seen as the defenders of new thinking. A leading advocate of this position was the outspoken journalist Aleksandr Bovin.[15] He was supported by senior Middle East specialists Vladimir Nosenko and Georgy Mirsky at the Academy of Sciences' prestigious Institute of World Economy and International Relations (IMEMO) and Sergei Rogov at the Academy's USA and Canada Institute (ISKAN), as well as Andrei Shumikhin at the same institute. They may have been joined by Sergei Bychal, aide to Valentin Falin, the head of the International Department and responsible (among other things) for the Middle East.[16] Eduard Shevardnadze's aide and head until 1991 of the Foreign Ministry's Division for Assessment and Planning, Sergei Terasenko, as well as Oleg Derkovsky, who replaced Gennady Terasov as assistant head of the Middle East Department with special responsibility for the Arab–Israeli conflict, were supporters of new thinking, along with the Deputy Foreign Minister responsible for the region, Aleksandr Belonogov, and others in the Planning Division.[17]

According to accusations voiced at an anti-Zionist demonstration, Primakov and above him Yakovlev were the main architects of the new policy towards the conflict.[18] Indeed, inasmuch as these two were largely associated with the theoretical underpinnings of new thinking, and Primakov himself was a Middle East specialist who as early as 1972 had advocated a different Soviet position on the conflict, they may well have been the leaders primarily responsible for the application of new thinking to the Arab–Israeli conflict.[19] In the power shifts of late 1990 to early 1991 Yakovlev and Primakov both emerged primarily as principal advisers to Gorbachev; but whereas for Yakovlev this represented a limitation of his previous influence and authority, for Primakov it was in essence an expansion of his importance. Primakov may well have become the most important figure in the determination of Soviet Middle East policy, although his official task from the spring of 1991 became the more important portfolio of foreign economic relations within the new National Security Council created by Gorbachev. Shevardnadze was, of course, the chief authoritative figure (along with Yakovlev) pressing for new thinking; this would include but not necessarily give high priority to the Middle East conflict. His replacement, veteran diplomat Aleksandr Bessmertnykh, devoted somewhat greater attention to the issue, and was also an advocate of new thinking, but he wielded nowhere near the same authority or influence as Shevardnadze.[20]

Effects of domestic factors

As a result of the debate and counter-pressures, therefore, the Arab–Israeli conflict became something of a domestic issue, unlike most other regional conflicts. In this sense, perestroika may have produced a situation similar to the well-known phenomenon in the United States, with a local lobby and interest groups rendering this a sticky domestic problem. And the fact that the opposition made this into an issue of perestroika (even Yeltsin took it up from the other angle, pushing for better relations with Israel and a crackdown on domestic anti-Semitism as steps on the path of more radical reform)[21] may well have given Gorbachev a further domestic interest in seeing an end to this conflict. While this may have operated indirectly as an added impetus for finding a solution, some of these same factors, namely the pro-Arab or anti-Israel pressures, were also the very factors that might restrain such an impetus, operating against Soviet disengagement and an end to the conflict. At the very least, they were compelling elements which had to be taken into consideration.

Israel

Despite such constraints, one of the first signs of the application of new thinking to the Arab–Israeli conflict was the change in Moscow's approach to Israel. Initially, the change appeared to be part of a merely tactical opening up, or improving, of Soviet relations with a variety of states normally aligned with or orientated towards the West. The purpose appeared to be to broaden Soviet options in the region, in order to enhance Moscow's position in the competition with the United States. Such a tactic was made possible by the changed attitude to Third World states – that is, the clause in the new Party platform, presented to the 1986 CPSU Congress, which called for favourable relations with capitalist states in the Third World. Israel thus appeared to be but one of the beneficiaries of this new tactic, along with Oman, Abu Dhabi and others. In the case of Israel, the tactic appeared to be merely a new means of serving an old objective, namely, a way of gaining access to the peace process and blocking a *Pax Americana*.

Normalization of relations

In time, however, it became evident that more than a change of tactics was involved; the moves towards Israel were part of new thinking, which included not only normalization of relations throughout the world but also, and in particular, resolution of regional conflict. Any genuine effort for a settlement had to involve Israel, and with the end of the zero-sum-game competition and the de-ideologization of foreign policy there was no longer a rationale, or need, for an anti-Israel position. In April 1987 Gorbachev publicly announced (in the presence of visiting Syrian President Hafiz Assad) Moscow's new policy of normalizing relations with Israel.[22] The announcement actually followed moves already initiated to deal directly with Israel, rather than unofficially or through the United States. Direct and official channels for communication were opened and relations were developed in a variety of areas, including, by the beginning of 1988, the exchange of consular missions, with political officers, on a temporary basis; cultural, academic, and sports exchanges; commercial talks; tourism; and even visits to the Soviet Union by ministers of the government of Israel.[23]

Israeli cooperation in the apprehension and return of Soviet hijackers in December 1988, followed by Israeli aid to Armenian earthquake victims, greatly accelerated the pace of normalization. Indeed normalization reached a level not far from the resumption of full diplomatic relations by 1989, when Shevardnadze included talks with Israeli Foreign Minister Moshe Arens (in Cairo) during his first trip to the region.[24] A symbolic culmination was reached in September 1989 when the Soviet Union finally abandoned its customary support for the annual Arab bid to have Israel's credentials revoked at the United Nations. This was followed by the agreement a year later to open permanent consular relations, a meeting between Prime Minister Valentin Pavlov and Prime Minister Yitzhak Shamir in London in March 1991, and the brief visit to Israel by Foreign Minister Bessmertnykh during his tour through the region in the spring of 1991.[25]

While all this fell short of the renewal of full diplomatic relations, presumably because of the domestic and Arab pressures mentioned above, Soviet conditions for such a renewal were greatly reduced.[26] They had often fluctuated in the past, becoming particularly demanding when the pre-Gorbachev leadership perceived little chance of actually becoming a party to Middle East negotiations. In the Gorbachev period there was a return to a minimalist Soviet demand (first expressed in 1973) simply for progress in the peace process, with only brief deviations from the line that Israeli agreement to even preliminary peace talks would be sufficient. Inasmuch as both Israel and the United States demanded renewal of relations with Israel as a condition for Soviet participation in any talks, Israeli agreement to some kind of Middle East negotiations (such as the Israeli–Palestinian talks in Cairo – with the USSR and the United States serving as observers – proposed by Baker in 1990, or the regional conference advocated after the Gulf War) appeared to be the catalyst that would produce the Soviet renewal of relations.[27] The decision for Bessmertnykh to visit Israel in May 1991 – the first such visit by any Soviet Foreign Minister – appeared to be timed to coincide with such a development in view of the then prevailing hopes that plans for a regional conference were soon to be finalized. As those hopes dwindled in the spring of 1991, the trip was made, but without any change in the formal status of Soviet–Israeli relations.

To persuade Jerusalem that Moscow had altered its attitude, hostile propaganda was generally replaced by more objective, sometimes even favourable, reporting on Israel in the government and Party media. The existence of glasnost meant that unfavourable reporting could still be found, particularly in the Russian nationalist papers and journals.[28] But as Soviet journalists became regular visitors to Israel, the Soviet media presented fuller, relatively unbiased accounts of Israel, portraying the complexities of the society and the nuances of the situation. The central press abandoned past comparisons of Israel with Nazi Germany and the identification of Israeli policy with fascism. Soviet support for the 'Zionism is racism' formula and the 1975 UN General Assembly resolution relating to this was also condemned as anti-Semitic.[29] In this context, it was admitted that Zionism was an ideology composed of several streams and varieties, including a social-democratic stream which definitely had positive features.[30] Such an admission marked an extraordinary departure from the traditional, blanket condemnation of Zionism that had characterized Bolshevik policy since pre-revolutionary days. Indeed, the Soviet permission for the convening of a Zionist conference in Moscow in May 1991 signified virtual (at least unofficial) acceptance of the movement.[31]

Soviet policy towards Jewish emigration

Also in part to convince Israel, Gorbachev undertook the improvement and freeing of Jewish life within the Soviet Union. Dictated perhaps largely by the social reforms connected with perestroika, as well as by a desire to satisfy American demands and to please Western Jewish businessmen, these steps were nonetheless also conceived in Moscow as confidence-building measures vis-à-vis Israel. They were apparently intended by Gorbachev as a substitute for, or a means of avoiding, a step which he did not initially appear to want to take: granting permission for Soviet Jews to emigrate. The theory apparently was that the expected improvement in the lives of Soviet Jews, along with those of all Soviet citizens, would eliminate the demands – from inside as well as elsewhere – for emigration. This of course turned out to be a miscalculation, leading to what rapidly became another component of the new Soviet policy towards Israel, the reluctant but gradual freeing of Jewish emigration.

Along with the renewal of diplomatic relations, the possibility of emigration for Soviet Jews had been a consistent Israeli demand since well before Gorbachev's decision to embark upon normalization. And an early, sporadic and greatly limited granting of exit visas to well-known 'refuseniks' was probably designed to placate without really fulfilling Israeli demands. Gorbachev was, however, under the added pressure of similar demands on the part of American and Canadian Jewish businessmen, upon whom he was counting to encourage joint ventures and investment for rebuilding the Soviet economy. Moreover, the Soviet position on this issue, and on freedom of emigration in general, became something of a test of perestroika in the eyes of many in the West, including and especially the US government; indeed, the United States continued to make the granting of credits and most favoured nation (mfn) status conditional upon the enactment of a law on emigration in the Soviet Union. These factors all combined to impel Gorbachev gradually to increase emigration to include virtually all of the refuseniks, finally bringing the total of Soviet Jewish emigration for 1989 to 100,000.[32] A massive exodus brought an additional 200,000 to Israel in 1990, in response to which, and at Israeli urging, the United States suspended its trade restrictions on the USSR.[33]

The unexpected push to leave was the result of the sharp deterioration in the Soviet economic situation, together with the alarming rise in popular anti-Semitism due to growing nationalism and the search by the Soviet public for a scapegoat for past and present hardships. Whether by traditionally anti-Semitic Russian nationalism, openly and often violently advocated by Pamyat', or by Ukrainian or Lithuanian or Islamic chauvinism, Soviet Jews became increasingly alarmed. Fuelled by the average citizen's resentment at the Jews' ability to leave or at the relatively high percentage of Jews among what were perceived as money-grubbing cooperative owners, anti-Semitism became a real threat as law and order broke down in the newly liberalized Soviet society. The alteration of American regulations for Soviet immigration to the United States effectively limited the numbers who could use this option, with the result that the fleeing Jews for the most part could head only for Israel. The massive emigration thus became an integral part of Soviet policy towards Israel.

The Israeli response

The Israeli response to the changes in Moscow concentrated on the realm of bilateral relations, and was primarily reactive. Jerusalem did take the lead in people-to-people contacts, cultural and commercial initiatives. In the political sphere, however, it focused on the renewal of diplomatic relations, insisting that since Moscow was the party that had severed relations, it was Moscow that must take the steps necessary for their resumption. This point of view, based on the conviction that the original disruption was an entirely unjustified, unilateral Soviet step, had led Jerusalem to maintain a studied indifference over the years to the various conditions raised by Moscow for renewing relations (conditions which had usually been connected with Soviet–Arab demands regarding the conflict). Israel considered these conditions only in terms of appraising the degree of Soviet hostility towards Israel at any given moment or, at most, the degree of Soviet interest in actually renewing relations. The reduction of Soviet demands was usually interpreted as part of the carrot-and-stick tactics designed to soften Israeli opposition to Soviet participation in the peace process.

Moreover, whether deliberately or not, Israel tended to maintain a clear separation between bilateral Soviet–Israeli relations on the one hand, and issues connected with the Arab–Israeli dispute on the other. Contrary to Moscow's efforts at linkage, Jerusalem denied the legitimacy of any such connection, viewing the existence (and renewal) of diplomatic relations as the normal, desired situation between sovereign states. Thus Israel was willing to go to an international conference with the Soviet Union in 1973 despite the absence of diplomatic relations, and it raised no opposition to the admittedly symbolic role played by Moscow in the signing of the 1974 disengagement agreements with Egypt and Syria, ostensibly within the framework of the Geneva conference convened after the war of October 1973. At the same time, Jerusalem studiously avoided any linkage of the conflict to the one bilateral issue of paramount importance to Israel, that of Soviet Jewish emigration. Jerusalem presumably sought to avoid the kind of blackmail Moscow might attempt by connecting demands for Israeli concessions in the Arab–Israeli context with Israel's deep interest in Soviet Jewry.[34]

Labour's response

A change in Israel's approach became apparent after Gorbachev began his first tentative revisions of Soviet policy towards Israel in 1985. Shimon Peres, then Israel's Labour Prime Minister, reversed Moscow's customary linkage by demanding that Moscow resume full diplomatic relations if it wanted to play a role in the Middle East peace process. He went so far as to allow for a Soviet role in an international forum, provided Moscow renewed relations, finally agreeing in August 1986 to the idea of Soviet participation in an international conference. Peres and Shamir, the then Foreign Minister, also introduced linkage of the demand for emigration of Soviet Jews with any Israeli agreement to a Soviet role in the peace process. This did not necessarily mean they were raising conditions in order to complicate the possibility of improved relations with Israel. It seemed more to be an effort, at least on the part of Peres, to take advantage of what was estimated to be a genuine Soviet interest in establishing a new, direct relationship with Israel – the new Soviet policy. The demand for linkage was, therefore, accurately based on the calculation that Moscow was ready to respond positively.

Peres, however, was not so much interested in improving relations with the Soviet Union as such, nor in granting Moscow a role. Rather, his was a more instrumental approach. His interest was in an international conference, for which it was necessary to improve relations with the Soviet Union. And the sole reason for the interest in an international conference was Jordan. The Labour Party had long subscribed to the so-called Jordanian option. Indeed, from pre-State days, Jewish leaders had been able to deal with or at least talk to the Hashemites, while other Arab leaders, especially the indigenous Palestinians, rejected any contact. Peres had maintained this traditional Labour preference for dealing with Jordan, and in the new Middle Eastern realities of 1986 Jordan was willing to negotiate with Israel only under the protective umbrella of an international conference. This then meant, for Peres, the need to agree to such a conference, and with it, as a concession to Jordan, Soviet participation; but there was also a price for the Soviet Union to pay. His position was therefore not the result of some sort of 'left-wing' sympathy for the Soviet Union. The classic if simplistic left = pro-Soviet, right = anti-Soviet stereotype did not fit Israel. In fact Labour had been traditionally anti-Soviet, in the pre-State years and the early years of statehood partly out of opposition to pro-Soviet political parties on its left, and later out of a genuine fear of Soviet military intervention. It was Labour that called a halt to both the 1967 and 1973 wars because of the perceived threat of Soviet military intervention. And it was Labour that warned against the risks of heightened tension in the region generally, emphasizing the need for moves towards peace because of the threatening Soviet presence.

Likud's response
The Likud Party, on the other hand, maintained a still more complicated attitude towards Moscow. Menachem Begin, as Prime Minister, had adopted the more expected generally oppositional right-wing/cold-warrior position. This was often dictated by a desire to please the United States as well as by his own propensity, perhaps, to condemn the Soviet Union. Yet even his own party, Herut, was less fearful than Labour of Soviet involvement in the region. For example, in response to the Soviet threat to intervene in the 1973 war, Herut held a more benevolent view of Soviet intentions and actions than Labour. In 1973 as well as 1967, Herut, under Begin, tended to minimize the threat of Soviet military intervention, while Labour (then in power) was believed to have agreed to a ceasefire because of fear of Soviet intervention. A minimalist view of the Soviet threat suited Herut's more aggressive policies vis-à-vis the Arabs, freeing the right-wing party from the constraints on military action invoked by Labour.

Shamir's response

Shamir, however, did not necessarily fall into this category of Herut politicians. Unlike Begin, he rarely, if ever, adopted a cold-warrior approach or anti-Soviet attitudes. The sources of his more benign position towards the Soviet Union may be traceable to his earlier role as leader of the radical pre-State Jewish underground movement, the Stern Gang (LEHI), which for a period was decidedly pro-Soviet. Born of hostility towards the British, the Stern Gang saw an ally in the Soviet Union and even went so far as to advocate the idea of a 'people's republic' on both banks of the Jordan.[35] Thus Shamir, unlike Begin (leader of the Irgun underground organization from which the Stern Gang had broken off) or even later colleagues such as Moshe Arens, did not subscribe to a traditional cold-war approach to Moscow. Rather, from his earliest days as Foreign Minister, Shamir sought improved relations with the Soviet Union, and at various times (in 1987 and again early in 1989) he expressed willingness for the Soviet Union to participate with the United States in sponsoring Arab–Israeli peace talks.[36]

Shamir was not entirely consistent, however, in his attitude towards the Soviet Union in the Gorbachev era, and he expressed often contradictory evaluations of the changes taking place in Moscow's policies towards Israel. His misgivings about the Soviet Union came to the fore during the period of intensive international (mainly American and Egyptian) efforts to convene Israeli–Palestinian talks, following Shamir's presentation of his own peace initiative. In September 1989, for example, he told a journalist that 'Glasnost seems to have skipped over the Middle East and has yet to reach Israel.'[37] Shamir dismissed the various steps taken in normalization over the preceding three years, calling the existence of consular delegations and other measures 'incidental'. He made no mention of emigration or the other components of the new Soviet policy. Rather, he pointed to what he characterized as Moscow's continued support for terrorist organizations and its special relationship with the Palestine Liberation Organization (PLO). These, he said, were dictated both by what remained of Leninist theory and by Moscow's continued interest in pleasing the Arab states. In answer to a question during the same interview, the Israeli Prime Minister also said that this policy barred the course of Soviet–American cooperation on the Middle East.

To some degree Shamir's comments reflected Israeli frustration over the continued absence of the long-awaited, oft-promised resumption of full diplomatic relations. More immediately, they may have been connected with a temporary cooling in the relationship that occurred over issues affecting Soviet Jewish emigrants – that is, Soviet responses to Arab pressures regarding the possibility of these emigrants being settled in the occupied territories (prompted by Shamir's comment that Israel needed territories to accommodate the large immigration).[38] At a deeper level, such inconsistencies suggested that the Israeli government was still in the process of weighing the impact of Soviet policy under Gorbachev and its implications for Israel and the Arab–Israeli conflict.

Shamir may actually have been addressing three broader concerns. First, a generally perceived softening of Soviet policies in the Third World, and specifically the idea of a Soviet pull-back from involvement with the Arabs, might create the impression of an eventual weakening of Arab military strength and, therefore, of less danger for Israel from its neighbours. This might lead to complacency on the part of Israelis, a reduction of the American (popular and official) commitment in the face of such a reduced threat to Israel and, concretely, a cutback in American military assistance to meet this threat.[39] Second, a belief that the Soviet position on the Arab–Israeli conflict had undergone a change, and that Moscow was seeking to moderate the Arabs rather than encourage their hostility towards Israel, might lead to the blame being placed on Israel for the lack of progress in the peace process.[40] And third, a reformed Soviet Union perceived to be pursuing a constructive, improved policy even with regard to Israel might be seen by Washington as no longer a danger to Israel, nor a cold-war competitor to the United States, and this might pave the way for concerted Soviet–American pressures upon Israel to acquiesce in an imposed Middle East settlement or, at the least, to agree to measures or procedures detrimental to Israeli interests.

The Gulf crisis

The outbreak of the Gulf crisis, however, heralded a fresh improvement in bilateral relations. This was accompanied by a return to a positive attitude on the part of Shamir, signalled by the meeting between the Soviet and Israeli prime ministers in London in March 1991. During the Gulf crisis Gorbachev took the almost unprecedented step of receiving two Israeli government ministers in Moscow and, more significantly, agreed in December 1990 to raise Soviet–Israeli relations to permanent consular level. Just as, earlier, Moscow had initiated a decided improvement in relations at the height of the Palestinian uprising or *intifada*, that is, at the peak of Arab and world criticism of Israeli policies in the winter of 1988, so too at a time of consternation in parts of the Arab world over Soviet opposition to Iraq, Moscow nonetheless chose to execute a step which could hardly improve its faltering status in the Arab world. Thus it appeared that the Soviet leadership had taken a decision at some point gradually to improve relations with Israel, and it simply implemented this decision regardless of events in the region.

The opening of consular relations during the Gulf crisis, however, may also have been something of a quid pro quo promised by Moscow as part of its commitment to the anti-Iraq coalition in exchange for a role in future Arab–Israeli peace efforts. Although the Soviet Union explicitly rejected Saddam Hussein's demands that resolution of the Gulf crisis be linked to settlement of the Arab–Israeli (and the Lebanese) crisis, the sequential linkage accepted by both superpowers, as we shall see below, promised Soviet–American cooperation in pursuit of a settlement; and the renewal of Soviet diplomatic relations with Israel was an American as well as an Israeli condition for Soviet participation in such a process. Therefore the Soviet government continued to move steadily towards such a climax, raising relations to consular level, conducting the prime ministerial meeting in London, later dispatching Foreign Minister Bessmertnykh to Israel in May 1991; the direction of the relationship was continuously upward. The final renewal of relations by Moscow would await the certainty of Israeli participation in some form of conference, which would thereby fulfil the condition Moscow had set presumably in order to justify the act of renewal to domestic as well as to Arab critics. In the meantime, Israel appeared to gain some popularity in the Soviet Union, partly because of its restraint (praised by Bessmertnykh) during the Gulf war despite Iraq SCUD attacks. Indeed the PLO ambassador to Moscow was to comment on the pro-Israeli attitude he perceived developing in the Soviet Union.

Syria

There was much in the new Soviet policy to arouse Syrian concern and criticism, from the Soviet *rapprochement* with Israel and the emigration of Soviet Jews to the internal Soviet debate over arms sales, in addition to many of the issues which had long been a source of disagreement between the two, such as Syria's presence in Lebanon, 'strategic parity' with Israel and control of the PLO. The primary Syrian concern was over possible Soviet disengagement from the Arab–Israeli conflict – that is, the possibility that Moscow would no longer be willing, or perhaps even able, to provide Damascus with the kind of political and military support it required for the pursuit of the conflict with Israel.

The Soviet withdrawal from Afghanistan, generally welcomed by the Muslim world, was viewed with some alarm in Damascus. Assad responded to a question on the subject with the comment: 'I think they [the Soviets] thought it was a good thing ... an outside observer might see things in an opposite way.'[41] A reversal of such magnitude, particularly in view of the enormous Soviet investment in lives as well as military and political effort on behalf of a Marxist regime bordering directly on the USSR, did not bode well for Soviet commitments further away to merely 'progressive' states like Syria in the Third World.

The crumbling of the Soviet empire in Eastern Europe and the disintegration of the Soviet economy did little to encourage Moscow's allies in Damascus, placing in doubt not only its will to stand by its clients but also the continuation of the trade and aid to which Syria had become accustomed from the Soviet bloc as a whole. The Soviets began to press for payment of the approximately $16.5 billion debt, initiating what appeared to be a cutback in arms deliveries.[42] The previous average of $2.3 billion worth of weapons per year fell to an average of $1 billion for the period 1985–9. Within this range, there were disagreements over certain advanced weapons, with the Soviet Union providing two squadrons of MIG–29 fighter aircraft only after some delay and at least one squadron of SU–24 bombers after even further delays (despite earlier sales to India and even Iraq). It refused altogether to supply SS–23 missiles, the production of which was actually banned by the INF treaty with the United States. There were rumours that Moscow might be helping Syria develop a chemical warfare capability when the Soviet army's chief of chemical warfare made two trips to Syria. The Soviets, however, claimed that the trips were connected with their concern over the proliferation of non-conventional weapons in the region, and indeed they may well have been concerned about the use of chemical warfare by Syria's neighbour Iraq.

The Soviet–Syrian arms deal

Serious difficulties in negotiating a new arms deal became apparent as Soviet and Syrian military officials exchanged a number of visits, reportedly with little success. Following a trip in 1988 to Moscow by Syrian Defence Minister Mustafa Tlas, for example, it was rumoured that the Soviet Union had refused Syrian requests for a wide range of advanced weaponry, from tanks to missiles to air defence systems and aircraft. The Soviets reportedly told Tlas that such supplies might provoke a pre-emptive Israeli attack. The issue was not only about the type of arms to be supplied, however. It was also, and perhaps mainly, economic, as was indicated by the visit to Damascus of the Soviet Minister for Foreign Economic Relations, Konstantin Katushev, at the close of 1989, reportedly to discuss Syria's repayment of its debt to Moscow.[43] According to rumours in the Arab world, Assad actually postponed a trip to Moscow scheduled for late 1989 because of these difficulties, and the negotiations for the 1990–5 Soviet–Syrian arms agreement, started in 1989, were painfully conducted and still incomplete two years later.[44] Assad's trip to the Soviet Union in April 1990 was conducted amidst continued rumours of differences in the military sphere, with Syria turning to China and North Korea for satisfaction of its demands.[45] The new Soviet–Syrian arms accord still eluded negotiators in February 1991, although Moscow did agree to reduce the debt by $5 billion. It refused, however, to offer new credits for arms.

The newly assigned Soviet ambassador to Damascus, Aleksandr Zotov, indicated that Moscow would be re-examining its deliveries to Damascus on the basis of economic feasibility, that is, demanding new as well as past due payments.[46] Explaining that the restructuring of the Soviet economy would entail 'new rules of the game ... [which would] affect in a certain way the modalities of our economic and other relations', Zotov told Western reporters that 'Syria's ability to pay' would, therefore, become a consideration. He added: 'Some of our complicated types of military equipment we prefer to sell for hard currency.'[47] Not only would economic considerations be given higher priority, but the new Soviet criterion for arms sales (as for its own military doctrine) would be, according to Zotov, the concept of 'reasonable defensive sufficiency'.[48] This meant sufficient supplies for the defence of Syria, but no more; there would not be arms for the achievement of 'strategic parity' with Israel, nor for the purpose of attacking Israel. This position was apparently outlined to the Syrians in various talks with Tlas and with Assad as early as April 1987, when Gorbachev announced the conviction that 'the reliance on military force has completely lost its credibility as a way of solving the Middle East conflict'.[49] The position was reiterated by Shevardnadze during his trip to the region in February 1989: the Soviet Foreign Minister remarked that 'more arms' did not constitute 'greater security'. Defence Minister Yazov also commented, just prior to a visit to Damascus in 1989, on the futility of the Middle East arms build-up.[50] He warned that the 'military capabilities in the region are much bigger than the economic and demographic weight of the Middle East on the international level ... [and] there is a real danger that the [global] disarmament process might be blocked by the absence of moves towards a just political settlement in the region'.[51]

Attitude to Moscow's Israel policy
From the Syrian point of view, these comments were all part of the diminished Soviet commitment to the Arab cause vis-à-vis Israel, as expressed by Moscow's espousal of a 'balance of interests' approach to the resolution of conflict. This strongly suggested a more neutral Soviet position; indeed, it was on the occasion of Assad's visit to Moscow in 1987 that Gorbachev chose to unveil his new policy of 'normalization' of relations with Israel. Even the appointment of Zotov as ambassador to Syria carried similar implications, for the Soviet diplomat, previously stationed for eight years in Washington and then assigned to Anatoly Dobrynin in Moscow, had been most active in liaising with Israel and in the efforts to improve Soviet–Israeli relations. President Assad responded that Israel had become 'the first beneficiary, among all nations of the world, of the international changes that have taken place', and other Syrian comments explicitly rejected the relevance of the balance-of-interests principle to the Middle East.[52] During Shevardnadze's visit in February 1989, for example, the Syrians argued that it was futile to try

to engage Israel in a diplomatic process, emphasizing Israeli intransigence while the Soviet Foreign Minister presented the view that:

> New thinking is powerfully knocking at the door of the Near East too. Through suffering, its peoples have achieved the right to a peaceful and safe life. It is time to build the bridges of mutual understanding and peaceful coexistence in this region too.[53]

The massive immigration of Soviet Jews to Israel was a focal point of Syrian as well as other Arab criticism of the new Soviet approach to the Middle East. Although they were undoubtedly concerned about the specific contribution the immigration would make to Israel's determination and ability to remain in the occupied territories, the Syrians seemed to be venting all their stored-up anger over a whole range of issues when they took Moscow to task on emigration.[54] Nevertheless, the Soviet leadership did not alter its policy on this issue, making only a minor concession to its Arab (and domestic) opponents.[55]

Lebanon and other issues

A number of other aspects of Gorbachev's policy in the Middle East initially provoked consternation in Damascus, such as the Soviet–Egyptian *rapprochement* and the continuing improvement in Soviet–Iraqi relations.[56] Nor were the Syrians pleased with Moscow's role in the reunification of the PLO and efforts to end Syria's hostility to its leader, Yasser Arafat (including Shevardnadze's futile attempt to hold a meeting with Arafat in the Syrian capital during the Soviet Foreign Minister's 1989 visit). Also of concern were the Soviet efforts, essentially for the first time, to bring about a resolution of the crisis in Lebanon. Moscow had played only a very minor role in connection with this country over the years, and both before and after Gorbachev's ascent to power it was not particularly pleased with Syria's intervention and growing domination there. Virtually ignoring the Syrian role, Moscow maintained its own, direct channels to the government and to various factions in Lebanon, occasionally even snubbing senior Syrian representatives in Beirut. Under Gorbachev, overt criticism of Syrian policy towards Lebanon was expressed: Moscow urged the Syrians to demonstrate greater openness towards the various factions vying for political power there. Moreover,

Moscow made it quite clear that Syria was operating on its own in Lebanon, privately suggesting that Washington might be more interested in the Syrian role than Moscow was.

In the spring of 1989 the Soviet Union began to take a more active stance, and one which was not, initially at least, to the liking of Damascus. At the time, Syria was directly engaged in the war in Lebanon, bombarding the forces of General Michel Aoun, who was supported by both Iraq and France. The Soviet Union, far from aiding this Syrian effort, joined international efforts to achieve a ceasefire, which was also to include the withdrawal of all foreign forces from Lebanon. This was hardly a demand that would be welcomed by Damascus. Nevertheless, in an unprecedented Soviet move on the Lebanese crisis, Shevardnadze issued a joint statement with US Secretary of State James Baker in May 1989 calling for just such a ceasefire.[57] Two months later, Bessmertnykh, then First Deputy Foreign Minister, was dispatched to Damascus and Baghdad to urge a ceasefire, having told the Arab League that Moscow would press for an end to the violence in Lebanon. During his visit to France, Gorbachev joined President François Mitterrand in a statement expressing 'profound concern at the continuing crisis' in Lebanon and urging 'an immediate ceasefire'. Going a step further, the two presidents called for an end to arms supplies from outside parties (read Moscow's two warring allies, Syria and Iraq) and expressed support for Arab League efforts to bring about a ceasefire (against the will of Syria).[58] Moscow then sought to prevent a planned Syrian ground assault on Aoun's forces by sending Terasov to the area in a shuttle between Syria, Lebanon, Iraq and Jordan, which included meetings with Christian (Aoun) as well as Muslim forces in Lebanon. Terasov reportedly brought Soviet ideas for solving the Lebanese problem, but basically Moscow was pressing for a resumption of the Arab League's mediation efforts, which did indeed resume shortly thereafter. This Soviet intervention may actually have prevented a Syrian offensive in Beirut at that time; there were reports that Terasov obtained Syria's agreement to limit its troops to the Be'qa valley in eastern Lebanon as part of a Lebanese peace accord.[59]

The most significant aspect of the intervention was the new Soviet activism with regard to Lebanon, in concert with the West and against Syrian interests. A second joint communiqué between Shevardnadze and

Baker, in September 1989, called for the preservation of the sovereignty, territorial integrity and independence of Lebanon.[60] At this time, however, an accord (the Ta'if agreement) had been achieved by the Arab states, and the Soviet position became closer to that of Syria, at least with regard to General Aoun, who had been delegitimized following the election of Elias Hrawi as President of Lebanon. Thus although the Soviet media reported Aoun's demands for the withdrawal of Syrian forces, they now also reported Hrawi's support for Syria's role. Gradually during 1990 criticism of the Syrians in Lebanon disappeared, and in October a Soviet Foreign Ministry statement justified Syria's intervention as a response to the request of the 'legal Lebanese government'.[61] This was a position which agreed with that of the United States and, following the Ta'if accord, most of the Western and Arab world. Later, the Soviets joined in the general support for the Lebanese–Syrian agreement of May 1991. This agreement sealed Syrian influence over Lebanon while bringing an end, finally, to the civil war in that country.

Reorientation of Moscow's Syria policy

While many of the signs of a new Soviet attitude towards Syria did lead to a deterioration in Soviet–Syrian relations, they were not necessarily an indication of a willingness entirely to abandon the Soviet relationship with Damascus. Syria was still Moscow's only state ally in the context of the Arab–Israeli conflict and an important element in whatever negotiations or accord Moscow hoped to bring about. Moreover there were strong forces in Moscow that wished to see the maintenance of Soviet military interests in the region in competition with the United States there. Thus despite the differences over arms supplies, the Soviet Union did indeed continue deliveries, meeting many, possibly most, of Damascus's requests, at the rate of $1 billion per year. Moscow also maintained close political contact and sought to reassure the Syrians that it would not neglect their interests, particularly with regard to defence.

Yet Gorbachev clearly placed the continued relationship with Damascus on a new basis, virtually oblivious to Syria's complaints and dissatisfaction. Moreover, he appeared undaunted, possibly even satisfied, that Assad responded to the difficulties by apparently beginning a reorientation in Syrian foreign policy. This included the reopening of Syrian–Egyptian relations in 1989 and a warming of relations with the United

States in 1990. With the end of the zero-sum-game approach, Gorbachev seemed to feel little concern over such developments and even praised the Arab decisions which brought US–Syrian cooperation in the Gulf crisis.

The Gulf crisis, however, greatly strengthened conservative forces inside the USSR, as we shall see in Chapter 5, and possibly precipitated a slight alteration of this position. As the forces favouring greater Soviet concern for the maintenance of power and influence in the Arab world became stronger in Moscow, the Soviets sought to assure Damascus that their alliance with Syria and support for its positions remained unchanged. This was basically the message Bessmertnykh sought to convey to Assad in Damascus in May 1991, but it did not appear to be backed up by concrete deeds. The 1990–5 arms deal remained in the stage of negotiations and the $2 billion that Syria received from Saudi Arabia during the Gulf crisis for the purchase of arms appeared to be going to North Korea and China for missiles, and Czechoslovakia for tanks.[62] The Soviet Union was still unwilling to extend new credits, and in fact sought repayment of the monies still owed. Moreover, following talks with Baker in Cairo, Bessmertnykh agreed to return to Damascus for a second time during his May 1991 tour of the region, in what appears to have been an attempt to press Syria to reach a compromise with Israel over the opening of peace talks. Thus Moscow did not appear to have abandoned any of the positions that had been the source of some strain in its relationship with Damascus.

The PLO

The change in Soviet thinking on regional conflict in general and on the Arab–Israeli conflict in particular clearly affected the Soviet–PLO relationship as well. This relationship had never been a smooth one, serious differences of opinion having marked mutual exchanges for years. Moscow had pressed the Palestinians even more than the Syrians to moderate their positions so as to become acceptable actors on the international scene, only gradually finding a common ground for support of most PLO objectives. As was the case generally in Soviet relations with national liberation movements, Moscow's interest in the movement had been of a highly tactical nature. Indeed Soviet support for the PLO had increasingly become a function of the Soviet–American competition as Moscow exploited the Palestinian issue, perceiving it as the Achilles heel of American policy in the Middle East.[63] This tactical or instrumental approach had placed limits on Soviet support and involvement with the movement, even as it dictated greater attention than Moscow might otherwise have accorded the organization.

Under new thinking, therefore, the PLO could expect a substantial change in the Soviet attitude on two accounts. At the more general level, an end to the zero-sum-game approach and the de-ideologization of foreign policy spelled a reduction of support for national liberation movements, including also support rendered for the conduct of armed struggle and terrorism. In this specific case, the fact that Soviet support for the PLO was directly related to the competition with the United States even within the context of the Soviet interest in the regional conflict (and this interest itself was linked to the superpower competition) meant that there was little hope that such support would continue. In theory, at least, disengagement from the Arab–Israeli conflict would mean disengagement from the Palestinians altogether. Yet its interest in resolving the conflict could also lead Moscow to maintain, rather than abandon, its involvement with the Palestinian issue, presumably out of a conviction that a lasting settlement would probably be impossible without resolution of this issue.

Early changes
In fact, just as the change in Soviet–Israeli relations had begun as a tactical move with the same pre-Gorbachev goals of merely improving Moscow's bargaining position, so too the attitude towards the PLO in the first two years of Gorbachev's rule continued to reflect a good deal of 'old thinking'. Gorbachev came to power in the midst of a very serious Soviet–PLO (or, more specifically, Soviet–Arafat) dispute. This dispute had been generated by the strife within the PLO (including a Syrian-supported rebellion within Arafat's own Fatah) following the strengthening of the 'rejectionist' forces (those opposed to settlement or negotiation with Israel), on the one hand, as a result of the Lebanon war, and the shift towards Jordan by Arafat and moderate forces, on the other. By conducting the Palestine National Council (PNC) meeting in Amman in 1984 and then signing an accord with King Hussein in February 1985,

Arafat had adopted a strategy designed to engage the PLO with the United States, in an effort to bring about a political settlement with Israel.

Although the Soviets, even before the rise of Gorbachev, had had little objection to the idea of a political settlement, they did oppose what was clearly a move by Arafat towards the Americans, perceiving it in the old terms of zero-sum competition with the West. Yet they did not support the rebellion against Arafat, nor the split within the PLO, for a number of reasons. The split – and/or the likely Syrian takeover of the organization – threatened to cripple, if not totally eliminate, the Palestinian movement as an effective actor on the Middle East scene. It would also strengthen rejectionist positions, which had little to offer the Soviet Union, while augmenting Syria's power to maintain its independence from Moscow.

The Soviet answer to this dilemma, therefore, was to counsel against a formal split and press for reconciliation while, nonetheless, virtually severing relations with Arafat's Fatah. Moscow apparently even sought a replacement for Arafat prior to the abandonment of the PLO–Jordanian agreement early in 1986 (for reasons not associated with the Soviet Union). It then vigorously mediated the reunification of the PLO that occurred at the April 1987 PNC meeting in Algiers. The meeting also formally abrogated Arafat's pact with King Hussein of Jordan and, as a gesture to Moscow, accepted two Soviet supporters (one communist and one fellow-traveller) onto the PLO executive.[64]

Public shifts

It was just at this time that Gorbachev was announcing to Assad the application of new thinking to the Arab–Israeli conflict, in his pronouncements that there could be no military solution to the conflict and that there should be a normalization of Soviet–Israeli relations. Indeed, both Israel and Syria were beginning to get a taste of new thinking, which was gradually to be applied to the Palestinians as well. The first public sign of the change occurred during Arafat's visit to Moscow in April 1988, when, according to the Soviet report, Gorbachev counselled the PLO leader to accept Israel's right to recognition and security, along with the Palestinians' right to self-determination, in keeping with the balance-of-interests principle. This became the thrust of a subsequent concerted effort on the part of the Soviet Union to persuade the PLO officially to recognize Israel's right to exist. Both George Habash and

Nayif Hawatmeh, leaders of the small Marxist factions, the Popular Front for the Liberation of Palestine (PFLP) and the Democratic Front for the Liberation of Palestine (DFLP) respectively, were invited to Moscow in September and October. The Soviets prevailed upon them to agree to UN Security Council Resolution 242 (that is, Israel's right to exist within secure borders) in order to advance the possibility of a political solution to the Arab–Israeli conflict.[65] A Fatah delegation also visited Moscow in October following a visit to PLO headquarters in Tunis by Polyakov, then director of the Foreign Ministry's Middle East Department.

This flurry of activity was designed to moderate PLO positions prior to the November 1988 meeting of the PNC in Algiers. Indeed, despite Palestinian denials of Soviet pressures at the time, Moscow was later to admit, even proudly claim, that it had played a role in the PNC's adoption of new, moderate positions regarding Israel.[66] While it was probably the impact of the *intifada* in the occupied territories more than these Soviet pressures that prompted the new programme adopted at the PNC, the PLO was subjected to a heavy dose of Soviet advice designed, from Moscow's point of view, to generate a new peace process. What Moscow was less enthusiastic about was the intention of the PLO to declare the creation of a Palestinian state at the same PNC session.[67] Moscow's motives were most probably connected with the desire to maintain a maximum of open and flexible options on the way to resolution of the conflict, so as to induce Israel to enter a negotiating process. Therefore the Soviets counselled the PLO to preserve the creation of a state as an objective, without seeking a *fait accompli*. When this part of their advice was ignored by the PNC, the Soviets were somewhat slow in recognizing the newly declared state, merely acknowledging the declaration and only belatedly – and quietly – officially changing the status of the PLO office in Moscow to that of a fully-fledged embassy in January 1990.[68] To avoid the complications obviously created by the proclamation of the state, Moscow cooperated in the effort to prevent this new entity from joining the UN or the World Health Organization, in 1989.[69]

The Soviet Union was satisfied, however, with the two major decisions adopted by the PNC and embodied in its new programme: the condemnation of the use of force or terror, and the acceptance of UN Security Council Resolution 242. The Soviet Union's attitude towards the use of terror by the PLO had been a mixed one all along, inasmuch as it traditionally preferred the use of political means over armed struggle for national liberation movements, and conventional rather than guerrilla warfare if armed struggle were adopted, disdaining the use of terror altogether on the grounds that it was counter-productive.[70] This had not meant in the past that Moscow did not support movements – by means of training, supplies, logistics, technical assistance – in their conduct of armed struggle and even terrorism. It did mean, however, that it had had an ongoing argument with the PLO as well as other movements over this issue and had sought to direct their armed actions against military targets and to convert their forces from guerrilla to regular army-type formations. Thus in the Brezhnev era, for example, a clearly terrorist operation by the PLO tended to provoke public condemnation by Moscow, tempered either by an attempt to portray the act as a guerrilla attack against a purely military target or at least by expressions of understanding regarding the motives involved, if not sympathy for the act itself.

Under Gorbachev there was a shift in Soviet policy from merely preferring political to armed struggle towards an exclusive reliance on political means.[71] And with this came outright condemnation of PLO operations 'whatever the motivation', and their unequivocal labelling as acts of terrorism. Palestinian 'extremists' who still advocated violence and terrorism were increasingly criticized in the Soviet media. More importantly, the Soviet Union began to cooperate with international efforts to curb terrorism, in part out of the desire to present itself as a responsible part of the international community. Moscow not only sought to play such a role but also began to limit its own support, ordering the closing of Abu Nidal's offices in Eastern Europe, for example, and gradually reducing if not actually terminating its own training and arming even of mainstream PLO groups. Thus it discouraged armed incursions into Israel from Palestinian groups in Lebanon, including groups close to Moscow such as the DFLP (both before and after the split within that organization).

Moscow was also careful to make a distinction between armed struggle and the *intifada*, which began in December 1987. Indeed the *intifada* was praised for its restraint and rejection of the use of arms, and the Soviet media tended to highlight its use of strikes, demonstrations and stone-throwing rather than the more dangerous 'Molotov cocktails' or stabbings. Yet the increasingly free Soviet press did contain negative as well as positive evaluations of the efficacy of the *intifada*, and official pronouncements paid surprisingly little attention to the uprising. This lends credence to the conclusion that, under Gorbachev, Moscow placed still less emphasis on even unarmed rebellion in the occupied territories than on political measures in the broader arena.

It was to facilitate these political measures that the Soviet Union was particularly satisfied with (and instrumental in achieving) the other major aspect of the PLO's 1988 programme: acceptance of UN Security Council Resolutions 242 and 181. These resolutions embodied the principle of partition: that is, the two-state solution and the explicit recognition of Israel's right to exist within secure borders. This was the balance of interests Gorbachev was advocating, and the key, presumably, to the initiation of Israeli–Palestinian negotiations. It was also the key to engaging not only Israel in negotiations but also the United States. The PLO's acceptance of Resolution 242, along with the renunciation of terrorism, had been conditions set by the United States in the past; with the PNC decisions Washington agreed to open a dialogue with the PLO.

The Soviet response to the American–PLO dialogue was a clear sign of just how far new thinking had come. Attempts by Arafat to open talks with the Americans in 1985 had led to a major rift between Moscow and the Palestinian leader; in 1988 the move towards Washington was welcomed and supported by the Soviet Union. Indeed when the dialogue was suspended by Washington following the terrorist attempt against Israel in June 1990 by the forces of PLO executive member Abul Abbas, the Soviet media regretted the suspension. Moscow even implicitly justified Washington's response in a letter to Arafat reportedly urging 'a rational policy' on the grounds that terrorist operations would be harmful to the peace process.[72] Similarly, it sought to persuade the PLO to accept the various ideas pursued for the convening of Israeli–Palestinian talks, including proposals by US Secretary of State Baker which allowed for only indirect PLO participation in talks to be held in Cairo between Israel and Palestinians from the occupied territories (unofficially chosen by the PLO). These talks never took place, because of Shamir's opposition to the participation of Palestinians from East Jerusalem. It was not entirely clear, however, whether Gorbachev would agree to the exclusion of the PLO at a formal peace conference, although there was little reason to believe that he would be any more willing than his predecessor, Brezhnev, to permit this issue to impede the convening of the long-sought conference. There were numerous comments and hints, particularly after the Gulf war, that Moscow favoured a solution to PLO participation in the form of a joint Arab or even joint Jordanian–Palestinian delegation, and that it urged the organization to be flexible.

The Gulf crisis

The Gulf crisis, in which the PLO sided with Saddam Hussein, did little to alter the overall cooling in the relationship. There were numerous trips to Moscow by PLO figures during the crisis, and the Soviet media barely mentioned Arafat's support for Saddam. Indeed those in the media associated with the more conservative position regarding the *rapprochement* with Israel and/or anti-perestroika positions actually sought to defend the PLO's stance, themselves urging direct linkage of the Gulf and Palestinian conflicts, as demanded by Saddam. Such a sympathetic attitude, however, was generally absent from official pronouncements. This may help to explain why Arafat refused to meet with Shevardnadze in Turkey when the Soviet Foreign Minister was on his way home from meetings in Washington (including one with Shamir) in December 1990. Nonetheless, primarily to demonstrate that relations were back to normal, Arafat and Bessmertnykh did meet in Geneva after the Gulf war, at the close of Bessmertnykh's visit to the Middle East in May 1991.

In fact relations were not back to normal following the war. The Soviet media carried reports of demands for Arafat's replacement, including comments from senior Soviet commentators critical of his decisions to support Saddam and encourage attacks on Israel. Not only was Arafat's leadership questioned but, for the first time, Soviet media carried comments challenging the PLO's position as the sole legitimate representative of Palestinian interests.[73] This did not necessarily reflect any official Soviet decision, and conservative elements continued to defend the PLO as such, but there were increasing signs that Moscow might be seeking some diversification of its contacts with the Palestinians. Aleksei Chistyakov, Soviet Consul-General in Israel, told an interviewer: 'We have found that there is room and possibilities for cooperation between us and the Palestinians in the occupied territories. We have just started this cooperation now and we intend to pursue it.'[74] This approach was in keeping with American contacts with Palestinians from the occupied territories (approved by the PLO, albeit after some initial reluctance), and the increasing likelihood of a joint Jordanian–Palestinian delegation for peace talks.

The Palestinians were not particularly pleased with the changes that occurred in their relationship with Moscow. Even more than the Syrians, they suffered from the loss of such important East European supporters as Czechoslovakia and East Germany. It is difficult to know at what point these losses began to affect the PLO's operational capability, but even at the political level East European and Soviet assistance could no longer be counted on. Even the day-to-day nature of the relationship with Moscow changed, as perestroika reduced the involvement of the Party in foreign affairs, shifting treatment of the PLO from the sympathetic care of the (now greatly reduced) International Department of the Central Committee to the more formal, business-like treatment of the Foreign Ministry. While the PLO maintained its access to leading circles, the nature of these Soviet contacts went from supportive to demanding to virtually neutral, at least as viewed from the Palestinian side. And the increasingly free Soviet media presented startlingly frank, often negative or critical portrayals of the PLO.[75]

Despite denials by some Palestinian leaders, concern was expressed by Palestinians and other Arabs over what was viewed as a contraction of the Soviet commitment to the Palestinians' cause, to the benefit of Israel and the warming Soviet–Israeli relationship. The Council of Arab Ambassadors in Moscow apparently raised the issue with Polyakov, the then Foreign Ministry Middle East Department chief, who had assured them in January 1989 that the 'Soviet Union continues to support the Arab causes, foremost the Palestinian cause'.[76] Ahmad Jibril, for example, openly called upon Moscow to return to its former positions and reconsider its new policy, which, he said, 'worries us'.[77] Soviet officials and commentators also indicated that there were Palestinian complaints or 'doubts', such as those expressed at a conference on the *intifada* held in Libya, at which critics apparently failed to understand Moscow's new, realistic policies; or at a symposium in Cairo, during which the Soviet delegates were questioned as to whether new thinking entailed settlement of regional conflicts only at the expense of Soviet support for national liberation movements.[78] A *Pravda* correspondent explained the situation:

'Let's be frank: the new ideas in Soviet foreign policy have confused some of our traditional close friends', adding that Arab and Soviet positions simply did not fully coincide.[79] Intending to dismiss rumours of difficulties, Foreign Ministry spokesman Gennady Gerasimov actually revealed the fact that Arafat's annual trip to Moscow had been 'skipped' in 1989 (nor did it take place in 1990), when he said that 'despite the lack of a recent visit to Moscow by Mr. Yasser Arafat', full support was still being given to the PLO.[80]

Such denials, on both sides, disappeared during the Gulf war, when Gorbachev himself alluded to the dissatisfaction in some Arab quarters, and PLO executive member Abdallah Hourani characterized Moscow's behaviour as 'an attempt to please the Zionist movement and obtain American money', concluding that 'it is no longer possible to regard Moscow as a friend and ally of world forces of liberation, including the Arab world and the Palestinian people and cause'.[81] The PLO ambassador in Moscow, Nabil Amr, took the Soviet media to task for what he termed its 'one-sided ... biased ... misrepresentation' of the Palestinians, and Arafat, generally cautious about even implying criticism of Moscow or admitting the existence of a problem, told an interviewer that, with regard to the Soviet attitude towards the Palestinian question, it was necessary to 'understand that there are international changes that must be taken into consideration'.[82]

The emigration issue

The openly acknowledged bone of contention was the emigration of Soviet Jews to Israel. An issue raised by various Arab countries, as we have seen, the massive immigration of Soviet Jews to Israel was of particular importance and concern to the Palestinians, who believed that this population influx would strengthen both Israel's will and its ability to hold on to the occupied territories. This fear was not diminished by Shamir's assertion that Israel needed the territories in order to absorb the large influx of immigrants.[83] A Palestinian delegation, including figures from the occupied territories, discussed the issue with Soviet Jews in Moscow as well as with the authorities in the spring of 1990, and the PLO sent an official memorandum on the subject to Shevardnadze in June of that year.[84] The memorandum warned Moscow not to accept

Israeli promises that the immigrants would not be settled in the territories; it called for a

> neutral international supervisory committee to implement the
> international resolutions to halt settlement in the occupied territories
> and to suspend intensive Jewish emigration from the Soviet Union
> to the occupied territories.

Thus the Palestinians urged Moscow to link emigration to the broader issues of the Israeli–Palestinian conflict and Palestinian rights, such as the end of Israeli settlements in the territories (including expropriation of houses, lands and water resources), the lifting of heavy taxes, the granting of freedom of movement and expression, the reopening of the universities, and other demands.

Despite the fact that Palestinian complaints were taken up by most Arab states and by domestic opponents to the Soviet *rapprochement* with Israel, the most Moscow was willing to do was to refrain from implementing an agreement for direct Moscow–Tel Aviv flights. Actually, as noted above, the agreement was eventually implemented, but direct flights of Aeroflot and El Al were limited to charter (round-trip) bookings which expressly excluded their use by emigrants travelling from the USSR to Israel. The Soviet Union also joined the campaign of countries (including the United States) demanding assurances from Israel that the immigrants would not be settled in the occupied territories. Gorbachev did threaten delays, even suspension of the emigration, if Israel failed to comply;[85] Bessmertnykh, too, responding to a press question in Amman, implied such a Soviet move. Yet upon reaching Israel, the Soviet Foreign Minister denied that any such steps would be contemplated and indeed it appeared most unlikely that these threats were more than a gesture to the protesting Arabs.[86] The whole issue was intimately connected with the sorely needed American trade benefits, specifically the granting of mfn status, which Washington had made conditional on the granting of free emigration. The passage in May 1991 of the long-awaited Soviet bill on emigration was a clear sign that Soviet priorities would not be altered by Palestinian or Arab protests.

Achievement of a settlement

The change in Soviet relations with the various actors in the Arab–Israeli conflict was accompanied by a change in the Soviet attitude towards both the content of a settlement and the means of its achievement. In the past, Moscow may not have been particularly interested, in terms of its own interests, in most of the substantive details of any settlement, such as the exact location of new borders or the fate of Jerusalem. Indeed there were a number of issues on which the Soviet leadership had rarely, if ever, expressed a position, for example with regard to the refugee issue or the Palestinian relationship with Jordan. Yet in keeping with Palestinian and Arab wishes the Soviet position on the issues, prior to Gorbachev, had become quite set in a standard three-pronged formula: the Israeli withdrawal from territories (sometimes called 'all the territories') occupied in or since 1967; the Palestinians' right to self-determination, including their own independent state;[87] and the independence, territorial integrity and security of all states in the region (sometimes explicitly including Israel).

Various peace plans presented by Moscow in the 1970s and as late as 1984 often also specified the return of East Jerusalem and the creation of the Palestinian state within the West Bank and Gaza Strip, along with a demand for the return of the refugees 'in accord with UN resolutions' – which meant return or compensation but, in the Soviet interpretation, tended to suggest that the actual solution of the refugee problem would occur once a Palestinian state was created in the territories evacuated by Israel. Details on such issues as Jerusalem or the refugees tended to appear, however, only upon the specific request of the Palestinians and in response to American successes – or approaches – vis-à-vis the Arabs. The means for achieving such a settlement was consistently declared to be an international conference of the type convened in Geneva following the 1973 war.

The impact of new thinking

With the new approach to the conflict and to Israel under Gorbachev, Moscow virtually abandoned this three-pronged formula and any details whatsoever. Both publicly and privately the Soviets made it clear to all involved that they no longer had any specific positions but, rather, would find acceptable any arrangements agreed upon by the parties to the conflict themselves.[88] The only principles they would specify were, in accordance with the balance-of-interests idea, those explained (publicly) to Arafat during his 1988 visit: Israel's right to security, along with the Palestinians' right to self-determination. Indeed, as far as the Palestinians were concerned, the actual demand for statehood tended to disappear into the more general formula of self-determination. As already noted, this did not necessarily represent a retreat from Soviet support for the idea of statehood as a Palestinian objective; it was presumably intended merely to open up the formula to interim proposals, and/or the possibility of Palestinian arrangements with Jordan, so as to engage Israel in a negotiating process. Actually the only details now offered by the Soviet leadership came with regard to Israel; that is, over possible arrangements designed to allay Israel's security concerns. These were presented by Shevardnadze during his trip to the region in February 1989, repeated during Assad's visit to Moscow in April 1990 and conveyed to Israel, the United States and, following the Gulf war, the Arab states. As outlined by Shevardnadze in Cairo, such arrangements would provide for the creation of a military risk-reduction centre to introduce and monitor a number of security measures for the whole region. These were to include limitations on arms deliveries to the countries of the region; control on the transfer of technology, particularly in the realm of non-conventional weaponry; nuclear and chemical disarmament; troop reductions and demilitarized zones; prior notification of exercises; international inspection and verification procedures; commitments against terrorism; and other similar measures.[89]

Although these ideas were proposed for consideration in parallel with rather than instead of negotiations for a peace agreement, they also contained, at least at one stage (before the Gulf crisis) a suggestion for convening a regional security conference. In the wake of the Gulf war this suggestion apparently merged with the idea of a regional peace conference, security arrangements becoming, presumably, one of the many regional issues to be settled along with the conflict itself.[90] Moscow did not officially abandon the idea of an international conference along the lines of the Geneva conference, but the parameters of such a conclave underwent several alterations and, eventually, total transformation. Even as they advocated an international conference, the Soviets increasingly spoke of preparatory talks, which could include bilateral as well as multilateral discussions, with or without UN and/or European participation. The conference itself would not be 'authoritative', in the sense that it would have no authority over bilateral arrangements reached between the parties, and would sit in plenary only to resolve issues unresolved in bilateral talks.

Gradually, however, Moscow avoided discussion of the parameters of a conference, referring more generally simply to the need for 'internationalization' of peace talks. This was the term employed by Gorbachev in the June 1990 summit in Washington, in which it became clear that Moscow was committed only to Soviet participation of some kind, rather than to any particular form of negotiations. What was important from Gorbachev's point of view, apparently, was the preservation of the Soviet Union's status as a great power and, therefore, Moscow's right to be a party to the resolution of regional conflicts (especially one so close to Soviet borders). Thus he sought inclusion of the Soviet Union in the Americans' peace-making efforts. Yet, by citing the example of former US Secretary of State George Shultz's consultations with Moscow (in 1989) as an example of the inclusion of the Soviet Union, Gorbachev appeared to be demanding no more than symbolic participation. In keeping with this position, the Soviet Union agreed to the limited role of observer, along with the United States, at the Cairo talks proposed by Baker in the spring of 1990, and expressed support for virtually every different procedure suggested by Washington or Cairo or even Jerusalem.

Postwar efforts

It was during the Gulf crisis that the United States finally consented to Soviet–American cooperation in what was to be the postwar effort for an Arab–Israeli peace.[91] From the Soviet point of view this was one of the principal positive results of that crisis, possibly even a quid pro quo for Soviet cooperation with the anti-Iraqi coalition led by the United States. When this cooperation faltered briefly in the closing stages of the war, there appeared to be a danger that conservative forces in Moscow, and in response also in Washington, might impede or significantly alter the prospects for such cooperation in the Arab–Israeli context.

In the postwar configuration of forces in Moscow, in which Shevardnadze, the authoritative champion of close cooperation with the

West, was no longer in charge of foreign policy, it was uncertain just what role the more conservative military and Party elements might play. These conservative elements apparently shared Gorbachev's understanding that Western economic aid was essential to the Soviet economy, and his interest in acquiring such aid, necessary for the modernization of the Soviet military. They also apparently shared his interest in stability in the region. It was not clear, however, how much they would regard these objectives as taking priority over their pursuit of the retention of Soviet power and positions in the Middle East, possibly at the expense of the relationship with the United States.

The emergence during the Gulf crisis of Evgeny Primakov as the central figure guiding Gorbachev's steps in the Middle East provided few answers. While Primakov was an important supporter or even formulator of new thinking, he was also an Arabist, sympathetic to the need to preserve a Soviet role in the Arab world. He may have perceived this role, however, as focused on the Arab states, including Jordan, as distinct from any particular interest in the PLO, but it was not clear just how far his interest in maintaining good relations and a Soviet role in the Arab world would take him in his policy recommendations. His transfer to foreign economic matters, which gave priority to relations with the West, may have affected his prior dispositions.

Despite Primakov's position, there was, in fact, little difference in Soviet policy regarding an Arab–Israeli settlement before and after the Gulf war (or before and after Shevardnadze's resignation).[92] In keeping with Moscow's intention of playing a role, Bessmertnykh made a visit to the region in May 1991. His inclusion of Israel in the trip indicated continuation of the new even-handed policy, while his consultations with Baker in Cairo and subsequent return to Damascus were signs of continued Soviet willingness to cooperate with American efforts and proposals; this was the same openness and flexibility that had characterized Shevardnadze's and Gorbachev's policy towards the conflict. Apart from publicly assuring the Arabs that the Soviet Union still supported their positions, Bessmertnykh adapted his comments and efforts to support the convening of a regional peace conference along the lines proposed by Washington, which were somewhat closer to Israeli demands than to the stated Arab positions. Once again, the details, framework and procedures were of little concern to Moscow; the objective was the convening of talks for resolution of the conflict, in concert with the Americans, and this was the message Moscow conveyed to the Arab states and the PLO.

In fact the Soviets began to speak of the need for a step-by-step approach, apparently accepting the Americans' concentration on achieving an interim agreement rather than a comprehensive settlement of the conflict. Bessmertnykh told an interviewer that it was

> most likely [that a] preliminary variant of the Palestinian problem will have to be worked out and, gradually, a final solution will be found, leading to a general settlement in the region. This means that the solution will be found step by step.[93]

Defending this position, *Pravda*'s Pavel Demchenko explained that tactics changed according to changing conditions but

> in fact, the tactics are aimed at the adoption of the shortest route to the achievement of strategic goals. Hence there is no reason whatsoever to be afraid or to describe the changes in Soviet–Israeli relations or the approval of the solution of the Middle East question by stages, as Baker has proposed, as retreat or passiveness.[94]

Soviet–American assurances to the Palestinians reportedly promised some future, permanent settlement of the Palestinian issue, but like Washington, and indeed supporting Washington's efforts, Moscow limited its interest to getting negotiations under way.

4

THE PERSIAN GULF

The Iran–Iraq war

There were contradictory signs with regard to the application of new thinking to the Persian Gulf area. The normalization and expansion of relations with states regardless of their social or political orientation significantly improved Soviet relations with Iran and the conservative Arab states in the Gulf. Yet this improvement could also be interpreted – and during the Iran–Iraq war there were grounds for such an interpretation – as an effort to limit the United States in a zero-sum competition rather than as the pursuit of cooperation characteristic of new thinking.

In fact the opening to conservative Gulf states even preceded Gorbachev by a few months, while an interest in Iran was by no means new.[1] Even under the Shah, Iran had been the object of many Soviet efforts not only to protect the long Soviet–Iranian border and limit, if not eliminate, the American presence, but also to expand the lucrative trade potential with the oil-rich state. The anti-American policies of the Khomeni regime had only encouraged these efforts, even to the point of some revision of Moscow's public position on the nature of Islam.[2] Thus Moscow refrained from taking an anti-Iranian position when its ally Iraq invaded Iran in 1980. The deterioration which had taken place in Soviet–Iraqi relations in 1978 and the potential presented by post-revolutionary

Iran combined to produce a neutral Soviet position in this war. Neutrality, in a conflict involving a country linked to Moscow by treaty (Iraq), amounted in effect to a pro-Iranian position; indeed, Moscow even suspended arms deliveries to Iraq as part of this ostensible neutrality. At the same time, however, Soviet offers of arms to Iran were apparently refused, and Moscow found itself increasingly spurned by Tehran. Once Khomeni destroyed and banned the Tudeh Party, expelled a number of Soviet officials, and rescinded its pipeline and energy agreements with Moscow, the Soviet Union shifted its support in 1982–3 back to Iraq (which was now defending its own territory from Iranian counterattack).[3] Although it did not completely disregard Iran, and permitted (perhaps encouraged) its communist allies in Eastern Europe and Asia to continue arms supplies, by the time Gorbachev came to power relations with Iran were in a very poor state.

The Iran–Iraq war had presented Moscow with a difficult situation, not only with regard to choosing between an erstwhile ally, Iraq, and a strategically and economically important neighbour, Iran, but also in connection with the US presence as a consequence of the war. Iranian victories had alarmed the basically pro-American conservative Gulf states, increasing the role of their Gulf Cooperation Council* and the military presence of the United States in the region for the protection of these states. In these circumstances Iraq, Egypt and the Gulf Cooperation Council states, primarily Saudi Arabia, were all drawing closer to one another and, potentially at least, to the United States. While this provided good reason for a Soviet interest in a swift end to the Iran–Iraq war, Moscow was nevertheless able to derive some benefit from the situation. It placed its own warships in the Gulf, to protect Soviet shipping, and responded positively to Kuwait's request in 1987 for Soviet protection by rechartering three Kuwaiti tankers. The Americans soon assumed this role for the Kuwaitis,[4] but a certain legitimacy for the Soviet presence had been achieved. More important, for Moscow, was the fact that Iran was increasingly in need of assistance as the tide of the war once again turned against it.[5] This provided an opening – at a time of US–Iranian strains, particularly over the Iran-Contra affair – which the Soviet Union was to exploit.

* This comprised Saudi Arabia, Kuwait, Bahrain, Qatar, the United Arab Emirates and Oman.

Thus under Gorbachev Moscow pursued a policy of improved relations with all the Gulf states, from Iran to Saudi Arabia. Relations with Oman and the United Arab Emirates were opened in 1985 and with Qatar in 1988. Existing relations with North Yemen were expanded both before and after the 1986 crisis in South Yemen. The Soviet Union was not involved in the conflict in Aden. It had supported the ousted leader Ali Nasir Mohammed (including his policy of improved relations with his conservative neighbours), and it initially sided with him in the crisis.[6] Even after shifting to the new regime in Aden and proffering aid, the Soviets encouraged the People's Democratic Republic of Yemen to continue the pursuit of improved relations with North Yemen as well as Oman, Kuwait and Saudi Arabia. This coincided with Soviet efforts to open relations with Saudi Arabia and Bahrain.[7] Indirect contacts were conducted with the Saudis in the form of visits to Moscow by Saudi figures acting on behalf of OPEC (by the Saudi Minister for Petroleum, Hisham Nazir, in January 1987) or the Gulf Cooperation Council (by the Saudi Foreign Minister in February 1988). The second trip, by Prince Saud al-Feisal (who was rumoured to be bearing a personal message from King Fahd) was actually the first step towards the resumption of relations, presumably agreed to in principle after Moscow had announced, on 8 February 1988, its intention to withdraw from Afghanistan within a year. The Afghanistan decision paved the way for a number of direct contacts, beginning in December 1988 and generally conducted by Yury Vorontsov, First Deputy Foreign Minister and then Soviet ambassador to Afghanistan. Soviet efforts were finally rewarded in September 1990, during the Gulf crisis, when both Saudi Arabia and Bahrain opened diplomatic relations with Moscow.

The expansion of relations with the conservative Gulf states was consistent with Gorbachev's new thinking. So too was the relatively cooperative and non-provocative posture towards the Americans on the part of Soviet warships in the Gulf.[8] Yet Soviet relations with Iran left some room for question as to Gorbachev's abandonment of zero-sum competition with the United States. It had been the Iranians, not the Soviets, who had precipitated the deterioration in Soviet–Iranian relations prior to and in the first years of Gorbachev's rule. And it was the Iranians who precipitated the amelioration which began in 1986, apparently in an attempt to break out of their own isolation and, eventually, to gain Soviet assistance. In February 1986 the Soviet Deputy Foreign Minister, Georgy Kornienko, visited Tehran and in August the Iranian Deputy Foreign Minister, Mohammed Laridjani, made a return visit to Moscow. These meetings culminated in an accord on economic cooperation signed in December 1986. Both sides were to gain from this accord, but most important for the Soviet Union was the Iranian promise to reopen the pipeline from Iran to the USSR; there were also reports of the return of some Soviet technicians to Iran following a trip to Moscow by Iranian Foreign Minister Ali Akbar Velayati in February 1987. More visits and commercial accords were to follow in 1987, along with increased arms shipments not only from Soviet clients such as Syria, Libya and North Korea but also from the East European countries, clearly at the behest of Moscow.

The improvement in Soviet–Iranian relations affected the Soviet position on the Iraq–Iran war, as was duly – and angrily – noted by Iraq. Moscow refrained from responding, for example, to problems with Iranian mines in the Gulf or to an Iranian attack on a Soviet freighter there.[9] More significantly, Moscow refused to support sanctions against Iran for the implementation of UN Security Council Resolution 598 to end the war. It also suggested the creation of a UN flotilla to replace foreign vessels in the Gulf. While this might be interpreted as part of new thinking's interest in reviving international bodies and collective solutions to regional problems, it looked much more like an effort to remove the American (and West European) naval forces from the Gulf. This would have relieved the pressures on Iran, in addition to serving Soviet interests in limiting the American military presence. Indeed the basis of the new Soviet–Iranian cooperation was a vociferous anti-American campaign.[10] Bypassing the Americans, Moscow tried itself to mediate an end to the war, dispatching Vorontsov to Tehran and Baghdad in the summer of 1987.

The *rapprochement* with Iran did not proceed entirely smoothly. The resumption of Iraqi missile attacks on Iranian cities, with Soviet-made SCUDs, in March and April 1988 aroused Iranian anger. It made little difference to Tehran that Moscow had opposed these attacks, having pressured Baghdad earlier, in the spring of 1985, to desist. Moreover, although the missiles had been supplied to Iraq by Moscow, Baghdad had altered their range so as to reach Iranian cities. This had angered Moscow not only because it threatened dangerously to escalate the war, but also because the apparently unauthorized adjustment (reduction of the warhead in order to gain a range of 650 kilometres) placed these missiles in the category of the INF treaty which banned the Soviet Union from producing such weapons.[11] At the time it was rumoured that the adjustment had been made with East German assistance, implying Soviet acquiescence; subsequently it emerged that the technical aid had come from West Germans. Nonetheless, in March and May 1988 there were demonstrations in Tehran against the Soviet Union in response to the Iraqi attacks, and Moscow responded with public criticism of the Khomeni regime for refusing to accept a ceasefire.[12] There were also signs of a reduction in the indirect Soviet arms deliveries to Iran (from Eastern Europe), leaving Iran with only China and North Korea as suppliers. Moscow now seemed prepared to cooperate towards the achievement of a ceasefire. The Soviet leadership may have calculated that Iran itself was now ready, in view of its serious defeat in the Faw Peninsula in April. The successful Reagan–Gorbachev summit in May was probably a central factor as well, leading as it did to a reduction of Soviet criticism of the US presence in the Gulf. Iran agreed to a ceasefire in July and peace talks began with Iraq under the auspices of the United Nations.[13]

On balance, the Soviets appear to have generally exploited Iran's anti-Americanism in order to improve their own position in Tehran but to have striven nonetheless to minimize damage to the emerging Soviet–American relationship. Therefore, despite hostile propaganda, the Soviet Union sought to limit its own naval presence in the Gulf and generally cooperated with the United States in this realm. The policy was one of political competition with the United States, which was greatly enhanced, for example, by Moscow's prevention of the imposition of sanctions against Iran. Yet Gorbachev was interested in an end to the war both to ease the tensions it generated and to facilitate broader Soviet aims with regard to the region as a whole and to superpower cooperation.

Postwar relations
The end of the war and the Soviet withdrawal from Afghanistan eliminated many of the remaining obstacles to the improvement of Soviet relations with Iran. Even before the death of Khomeni in 1989, Shevardnadze made a trip to Tehran (which was preceded by a visit to

Moscow by representatives of Khomeni), meeting with Khomeni in February 1989; this led to the expansion of economic and other relations.[14] A trip to Moscow by Hashemi Rafsanjani, heir apparent to the ageing Iranian leader, was planned at this time but implemented just a few weeks after Khomeni's death on 4 June, when Rafsanjani was the only candidate for the Iranian presidency.[15] It was during this trip that historic new accords were reached between the two countries in two days of talks between Rafsanjani and Gorbachev. Rafsanjani reiterated Iran's opposition to dependence upon any outside power, and Gorbachev presumably indicated Moscow's continuing concern over the messianic nature of Iran's fundamentalism and its effect upon Soviet Muslims or the situation in Afghanistan. Nonetheless, the major accords signed by the two countries included both a reportedly large arms agreement and a commitment by each side not to interfere in the internal affairs of the other. Rafsanjani also said publicly that Iran would not interfere in the internal affairs of Afghanistan either, despite its friendship with the Mujaheddin there, now that the Soviet army had withdrawn.[16]

Iran, too, had an interest in the non-interference clause of the new agreement, which was designed to prevent Soviet support for communist activity or for minority agitation, among the Kurds for example. Under Gorbachev, however, neither pursuit appeared to be of interest to the Soviet leadership. The problems were actually the other way around: that is, there was concern over possible Iranian activity among the agitated minorities on the Soviet side of the border, particularly in predominantly Shi'ite Azerbaijan. To allay such fears, Rafsanjani appeared in Baku's main mosque and praised Gorbachev personally for his reforms, especially in the area of religious freedom, referring to him as one of the world's great leaders. Yet six months later Moscow was to accuse Iran of playing a role in the disturbances in Azerbaijan which led to armed Soviet intervention in Baku. The Iranians were accused not only of providing moral support for the Azeris fighting Armenians in Baku or those seeking the independence of the Azeri enclave of Nakhichevan, located between Iran and the Soviet Republic of Armenia, but also of arming Azeri nationalists who were illegally crossing into Iran. The riots and demonstrations by Soviet Azeris were actually more nationalistic than religious, but demonstrators did carry pictures of Khomeni and they did swarm across the border into Iran, leading to Soviet accusations against Iran (particularly after the Ayatollah Ali Khamenei, spiritual leader of Iran and himself an Azeri, attributed the demonstrations to the Azeris' 'Islamic zeal').[17] Although comments like this were heard from hardline Iranians, official government statements exhibited restraint, because the pragmatists were in the ascendant.[18] The government in Tehran was presumably also anxious not to stir up Azeri sentiment in view of the effect this could have on dissatisfied Azeris in Iran, whose own grievances had not been met. Thus the issue had the potential for complicating Soviet–Iranian relations, but officially at least the accords signed in 1989 were honoured.

Quite apart from the prevention of outside interference in the difficult nationality issue of the Muslim Soviet republics bordering on Iran and concern over Islamic revival, Moscow had strong economic reasons for ensuring the implementation of the accords. Iran provided a promising market for Soviet industrial goods unable to compete on Western markets. Agreements were reached, for example, on the sale of Soviet commercial aircraft to Iran and on joint production of such aircraft. Soviet involvement in approximately twenty industrial projects in Iran was negotiated, along with the exchange of goods between Iran and neighbouring Soviet republics such as Turkmenistan and Azerbaijan. Iran was to export mainly consumer goods, as well as conducting joint projects along the Caspian Sea. The latter were part of the energy agreements signed between the two countries, providing for joint exploration and exploitation of Caspian Sea oil.[19] Moscow later sent a request for membership of OPEC, which was deemed likely to be granted.[20]

The economic accords of 1989 included agreements totalling some $6 billion over a ten-year period, 90% of which were to be covered by Iranian gas exports (3 billion cubic metres per year). These exports were also to cover arms purchases from Moscow, said to include the supply of 300 tanks, armoured vehicles and artillery, as well as anti-tank and surface-to-air missiles and some 200–300 advisers.[21] In fact the Iranians were reported to have a $20 billion shopping list for arms.[22] Following the Gulf war they sent a delegation to Moscow, led by the Iranian Air Force commander and, according to the Iranian news agency, negotiated an accord to purchase Soviet aircraft.[23] Indeed Soviet–Iranian relations, particularly in the area of trade and arms, were to improve still more in the wake of, and as a result of, the Gulf war.

5
THE GULF CRISIS

Soviet policy

Gorbachev's new thinking on foreign policy was tested, indeed stretched to its limits, in the Gulf crisis; it may have been stretched beyond its limits. Two periods could be discerned in Soviet behaviour regarding the crisis, the second corresponding to and reflecting the singular increase in the influence of conservatives from the Party, the military, and military industries. Their power was felt primarily in domestic affairs, most blatantly with regard to the nationalities issue, but it had also been gathering in the area of foreign policy, as was demonstrated both by Shevardnadze's resignation and by the difficult juggling act undertaken by Gorbachev as the Gulf war progressed.

Moscow's response to and initial behaviour following the Iraqi invasion of Kuwait was entirely in keeping with new thinking. Intent upon demonstrating that the Soviet Union was serious about belonging to the world community of responsible, law-abiding and cooperative nations, the Soviet leadership left the old ideological and zero-sum-game considerations behind and joined the American-led coalition against Iraq, a 'progressive' Third World state allied to Moscow by treaty. The Soviet–Iraqi alliance had long since been reduced to a basically commercial (and military) relationship, and the Soviet Union also had much to gain economically from siding with the West and conservative Gulf states such as Kuwait and Saudi Arabia. In theory, at least, they also stood to gain from the crisis-related rise in oil prices. Yet Soviet officials anticipated a loss for 1990 of approximately $800 million in trade and payments, primarily for tripartite oil deals between the Soviet Union and Iraq for deliveries to countries such as Bulgaria, Romania and India.[1] Anticipated losses also included non-payment of an Iraqi debt to the USSR unofficially estimated at anywhere between $5 and $20 billion.[2] Nor was the failing Soviet oil industry in a position to take significant advantage of the price rises caused by the crisis.

Early behaviour dictated by new thinking and apparently formulated by Foreign Minister Shevardnadze included the unprecedented joint condemnation of Iraq issued with visiting Secretary of State James Baker on 3 August and subsequent cooperation in the Security Council, which involved participation in the sanctions and suspension of virtually all official relations with Iraq except for those connected with the crisis itself. An interdepartmental committee created for the evacuation of Soviet citizens from Kuwait and Iraq, chaired by Igor Belousov, deputy chairman of the Council of Ministers and head of the State Commission for Military–Industrial Affairs, maintained contacts with Baghdad, sometimes combining its efforts with the high-level political attempts by Moscow to resolve the crisis. But even in their meetings with Iraqi leaders prior to the outbreak of war, the Soviets loyally represented the coalition position. This included explicit rejection of Saddam's proposed 'linkage' of withdrawal from Kuwait to the resolution of the Palestinian and Lebanese problems. The most Moscow would concede on this point was sequential linkage – that is, agreement that the Arab–Israeli conflict be tackled following resolution of the Gulf crisis. Sequential linkage, however, was advocated by the United States as well; it was urged by President Bush in his speech to the United Nations in September 1990 and in the joint communiqué issued after the September summit. The Soviets also expressly welcomed the decisions of the Arab heads of state to join the coalition force in the Gulf – decisions which meant that their own ally Syria entered into cooperation with the United States.

From the outset, however, the policy chosen by Gorbachev and Shevardnadze was fraught with difficulties, some stemming from new thinking itself as well as from opposition to new thinking. A serious problem was the possibility of the use of force if Iraq failed to withdraw from Kuwait. New thinking expressly opposed any but political solutions to crises, and the thrust of Gorbachev's foreign policy eschewed the risks of military conflicts and the use of the military in overseas ventures. Combined with the 'post-Afghanistan syndrome' in Soviet society and pressures from those concerned with maintaining Moscow's former alliances in the region, these constraints made it difficult for Moscow to support decisions calling for the use of force, let alone join in any military action in the Gulf. Gorbachev therefore delayed and sought to soften if not prevent the relevant UN Security Council decisions (Resolutions 665 and 678), permitting the use of force. However, in each case, following high-level attempts to persuade Iraq to retreat (in talks with Tariq Aziz for example), Moscow cooperated with Washington. It even agreed in principle to join a UN force should one be created – a move for which Shevardnadze was to be severely criticized, as we shall see below.[3] Such cooperation initially came after American assurances (at the Helsinki summit in September) that US forces would not remain in the Gulf on a permanent basis, but it was also possible to view Soviet cooperation as a quid pro quo for the American promise to include Moscow in Middle East affairs (specifically the Arab–Israeli peace process) and, later (perhaps), American toleration of the attempted crackdown in the Baltic republics.

Reformist pressures

The Gulf crisis unleashed a flood of domestic criticism and demands, focusing mainly on the fact that the Soviet Union had been the primary arms supplier to Baghdad. A Soviet poll conducted in September revealed that 38% of the population held Moscow at least partially responsible for the Iraqi invasion because of its arms supplies.[4] The earlier debate among experts erupted into demands for the cessation of the use of arms sales as an instrument of Soviet foreign policy, adding a moral issue to absence of profits from these 'sales' to Third World countries. As a frequent political commentator on Soviet radio, Igor Fesunenko, put it:

This situation has revealed the absurdity and unnaturalness of our frequent, so-called aid, especially military aid to Third World countries. This paternalism of ours, this feeding by us of frequently odious dictatorial regimes, which call themselves anti-imperialist and progressive, and on this basis alone we send weapons, money, food, anything there. ... More than once I have seen how this is done in deeds, how weapons are thrown about, in whose hands they end up – it is a terrible picture from every point of view. It is not just a matter of huge profits, because Angola, Ethiopia, Mozambique, Cuba, Cambodia, Vietnam and many other countries will never return even a small part of the expenditures on weaponry which we have supplied them.[5]

He called for parliamentary controls on such supplies, an idea raised in previous discussion and supported, for example, by Deputy Foreign Minister Vladimir Petrovsky.[6] An international register of arms transfers, also previously proposed, was advocated by Major-General Vadim Makarevsky – an indication that the military, at least, was not united in its defence of this trade. Makarevsky added the original point that Soviet security was now threatened by the 'South', those 'to whom the Soviet Union has sold and continues to sell (or to be more precise, has given and continues to give as presents) state of the art devastating weapons'.[7]

Criticism broadened to include all of Moscow's past policies in the Middle East (in which, it was claimed, any dictator or local leader who had merely learned to pronounce the word 'socialism' had been supported), the decision-making process and the continued influence of persons responsible for the past policies, and the lack of information as to who had authority to make decisions, for example, over arms deliveries and the precise quantities involved. The criticism reached the International Affairs Committee of the Supreme Soviet in an address given by Deputy Foreign Minister Belonogov. Belonogov himself later admitted that Moscow's 'entire concept of military cooperation with the countries of the Middle East has to be revised and conclusions drawn' in the light of the Gulf crisis.[8]

From the same amorphous 'pro-perestroika' camp came demands for the removal of all Soviet military experts from Iraq, parliamentarians of the Russian Republic taking this even further to the demand for abrogation of the Soviet–Iraqi Treaty of Friendship and Cooperation and cessation of the training of all Iraqis in the Soviet Union. There were many who explicitly championed American moves in the Gulf in response to

Saddam Hussein, and there were even those – from academia, the press and the general public – who urged direct Soviet participation, in the form of volunteers or the dispatch of at least a symbolic naval or medical contingent if not actual troops.[9]

Yet the vast majority of those supporting Gorbachev's policy on the crisis opposed the dispatch of Soviet troops in any form. A poll indicated that only 8% would have approved such an action.[10] And this fact was duly exploited by the opponents of Moscow's position on the Gulf. Gradually these opponents became the more vociferous, in some cases expressing deeper and broader concerns related to new thinking as a whole and to the future of Soviet power.

Conservative opposition

The most powerful opponents were the military and presumably also those involved in the military industries. They could argue a contradiction within new thinking itself between the rejection of military as distinct from political resolution of conflict, on the one hand, and the domestic economic need for arms sales abroad on the other. They were mainly concerned, however, over the loss of Soviet power, especially with the disintegration of the Warsaw Pact, and they saw in Gorbachev's Gulf policy a blow to Soviet power in yet another region. In the eyes of the military, not only were Moscow's positions in the Middle East and its potential for future power projection endangered, but the United States stood to benefit. These critics did not condone Iraq's moves, but they perceived the United States as using the crisis to establish a military presence in the Gulf, even as a replacement for the now untenable American military presence in Western Europe, and as a way of shifting NATO power against the Soviet Union to areas to the south of the USSR.[11] Gorbachev's vision of the end of bipolarity had, in their eyes, turned into American 'unipolarity' – and with Soviet assistance as well.

The military's concern over the blow to Soviet power was shared by conservatives of the Communist Party. Before his appointment as Vice-President, Gennady Yanayev, who was the Politburo official responsible for international affairs, complained in the Soviet parliament about the 'flabbiness' of government responses in the crisis.[12] This was the objection to Moscow's eclipse as a world power; its role was perceived as merely rubber-stamping Washington's decisions regarding the

Gulf. Russian nationalists, too, expressed their dissatisfaction; this was compounded by an element of anti-Semitism, which in any case opposed a policy that appeared to slight the Arab cause to the benefit of Israel. There was additional opposition from many Soviet 'Arabists' in academia and the press (although not, apparently, those in the Foreign Ministry). Many of these Middle East specialists were not necessarily opposed to new thinking as the military and party conservatives were, but they did object to what was viewed as disloyalty to Moscow's long-time allies in the Arab world. As experts, they maintained that the American presence in the Gulf would eventually produce an indigenous Arab and Muslim backlash, so they argued that it would be in the Soviets' interest to dissociate themselves from the Americans in the region. In this there was agreement with the military, who also worried over the future of Soviet positions there.

Effects on policy

For many involved in this debate the issue was one mainly of degree – that is, how to pursue new thinking without becoming a second-rate power or a mere appendage to the United States. For others, however, it was a question of priorities emanating from principles. On the one side was Gorbachev's and Shevardnadze's vision of the Soviet need for and interest in a strong relationship with the West, primarily the United States, in an interdependent world in which regional influence or positions would no longer be sought because of the end of zero-sum-game competition and the advent of international cooperation. On the other side was the conservative view of continued competition in the world and therefore the need for regional positions and influence, which took priority over – indeed could even be allowed to jeopardize – cooperation with the West.

Over the months of the Gulf crisis, the conservatives of the military and Party gained in strength. This was due primarily to the sharp deterioration in the Soviet domestic situation: the imminent collapse of the economy, the impending disintegration of the Union, the breakdown of law and order – in short the failure of perestroika. By the late autumn of 1990, Gorbachev was already making concessions to the conservatives, assuming greater central powers and permitting a freer hand to the security forces, presumably in the hope of creating a situation in which he could eventually enforce perestroika. Soviet policy regarding the Gulf crisis contributed, however, to the strengthening of the conservatives. Compounding, for the military, the humiliation and weakening of Soviet military power caused by the loss of Eastern Europe and disarmament accords with the West, Gorbachev's newest ostensible 'sell-out' to the West could be and was used to rally Party and nationalist forces. Popular sentiment could even be aroused through accusations that this policy of disregard for Soviet prestige and status in the world also included plans to send troops to fight in the Middle East.

Thus as major architects of perestroika such as Aleksandr Yakovlev and Leonid Abalkin became the victims of concessions to the military and Party conservatives on matters such as Baltic independence, economic reform, even elements of glasnost, Shevardnadze became the first victim in the realm of foreign policy. Under constant demagogic attack from the conservatives with regard to the Gulf policy, indeed actually undermined by independent and secret deeds by the military in the area of arms control (such as the shifting of certain weapons beyond the Urals so as to exclude them from the accords) and possibly also the Gulf (such as rumoured arms shipments to Iraq), Shevardnadze expressed his despair over the spectre of dictatorship and resigned on 20 December. With his exit, the way was open for subtle but significant changes in policy which gradually became apparent in Soviet behaviour once the war in the Gulf was under way.

Shevardnadze's replacement by career diplomat Bessmertnykh was in fact a positive sign promising the continuation of Shevardnadze's Middle East policies, which had been supported by Bessmertnykh in the past. But the new Foreign Minister lacked his predecessor's authority, especially against the rising power of Party conservatives such as Yanayev, the Politburo member responsible for international affairs, who was named Vice-President, and even Aleksandr Dzasokhov, Party secretary for ideology. While both of these sought a greater say in foreign policy, conduct of the Gulf policy fell increasingly into the hands of Middle East expert Evgeny Primakov. Though a supporter of new thinking, Primakov had nevertheless come into conflict with Shevardnadze as early as October over what he saw as the need to pursue a Middle East policy that was more independent of the United States in order to protect future Soviet interests in the Gulf.[13] It was Primakov who undertook a number of initiatives to prevent and later to end the war against Saddam, culminating in the last-minute 'Gorbachev proposals' for a ceasefire that were negotiated with Tariq Aziz in Moscow just before the ground offensive.

Signs of the change came during Bessmertnykh's talks with Baker in Washington at the end of January, when the new Soviet Foreign Minister cautioned the Americans against destroying Iraq rather than concentrating on the withdrawal of Iraq from Kuwait.[14] This was followed by what appeared to be a bid for a ceasefire launched by Gorbachev in order to prevent a ground war. He issued a statement which called for Iraqi withdrawal from Kuwait and condemned Iraq's effort to provoke Israel into the battle but also spoke of what Gorbachev said appeared to be moves by the coalition forces that went beyond the mandate accorded by the Security Council.[15] This statement appeared just a few days after a decision by the Communist Party Central Committee calling on Gorbachev to 'take the necessary steps' to bring about an end to the bloodshed.[16] It was accompanied by the dispatch of Primakov to Baghdad, on 12 February 1991, with what turned out to be a Soviet plan for a ceasefire and for Iraqi withdrawal from Kuwait. Primakov's plan was sub-sequently refined in talks with Tariq Aziz in Moscow on 21–22 February; these called for a ceasefire, to be followed forty-eight hours later by the ending of sanctions against Iraq, and an Iraqi withdrawal from Kuwait over a period of three weeks.

At the same time, there were increasing rumours of the continued presence of Soviet military advisers in Iraq (despite official Soviet denials) and of continued Soviet military aid to the country; there was even a report that Iraqi planes shifted to Iran had been transferred to Soviet air bases in Afghanistan for maintenance.[17] While these were for the most part only rumours, they may also have been signs of the increased influence of military circles in Moscow that were either conducting their own 'foreign policy' or forcing Gorbachev's hand in the interests of preserving Soviet positions in the Middle East (that is, a policy commensurate more with power projection than with new thinking).[18]

The ceasefire initiative was obviously a last-ditch attempt to head off the planned ground offensive, which Gorbachev had urged the Americans to postpone. More than this, however, it represented the supreme effort by the besieged Soviet leader to placate the demands of the conservative forces in Moscow, primarily his military, without seriously damaging relations with Washington. While his interest in preserving the relationship with the United States was clearly not shared by the military, Gorbachev may have believed that the arrangements for Iraqi withdrawal would be open to further negotiation by the coalition and that support from some West European countries such as France would minimize damage to Soviet–US relations. That Gorbachev was engaged in a juggling act to please domestic opponents in the hope of ultimately resuming his own policies was demonstrated by the return to full cooperation adopted by Moscow in the events that followed. Once the United States virtually ignored the Soviet plan and the ground war commenced, the Soviet Union joined with the coalition at the Security Council in dictating terms to Baghdad for a ceasefire and for compliance with all the Security Council resolutions.

Decision-making

It was, in fact, this domestic struggle that had dictated much of Soviet policy during the Gulf crisis, at times running contrary to new thinking, as we have seen. Yet the crisis itself was neither a central domestic topic in the preoccupied and troubled USSR, nor one which significantly altered Soviet decision-making, beyond the indirect connection with Shevardnadze's resignation. Glasnost was much in evidence, and it was clear that even in a time of crisis the media were now generally free. The democratization of decision-making, however, was far less evident. One expects decision-making in time of crisis, in any country, to be contracted and concentrated in the hands of the few, but in this case the lines of authority and the role of the various bureaucracies, institutions and decision-making bodies, as well as of public opinion and elected organs, were far from clear.

Within the Soviet parliament, the conservative group of Communist and nationalist deputies, Soyuz, was most active in the onslaught on Shevardnadze, exploiting his statements regarding the possible Soviet contribution to a UN force in the Gulf. The parliament and the Supreme Soviet were not particularly active, however, with regard to the crisis; this included even the International Affairs Committee, which might have been expected to monitor the decisions of the government. This committee did debate the Gulf situation after presentations by Deputy

Foreign Minister Belonogov. And it did hear samples of both sides of the public debate. Yet its resolutions dutifully supported the government's policy, with only the slightest hint of the varied and critical points of view expressed in its own deliberations.[19]

The International Affairs Committee also heard criticism of the Foreign Ministry for its failure to provide information and analysis of events with regard to Soviet state interests. The fact of this criticism was reported only by *Izvestiya*, which itself protested that Belonogov's presentation to parliament had contained nothing which had not already been available in the press.[20] The paper repeated this complaint later, with regard not only to the inadequate information provided to parliament and the public, but also to the failure of the Supreme Soviet itself to conduct a thorough debate of policy in the crisis. Criticizing the Committee's perfunctory discussion and approval of the government's policy, *Izvestiya* correspondent Vladimir Skosyrev bemoaned the fact that foreign policy remained in the hands of 'the top people in the state, the Foreign Ministry and other powerful departments', despite the numerous demands for parliamentary control over the formation of state policy.[21]

Voicing similar criticism, Bovin argued that many 'doubts and questions' would disappear if 'our super-departments – the Foreign Ministry and Defence Ministry – were to behave less coyly, if they were clearly to explain and describe the motivation behind their decisions and their positions'.[22] Also in *Izvestiya*, Stanislav Kondrashov presented a more nuanced picture, one of infighting between the two ministries. On the question of the military specialists, he said that in private discussions with 'senior staff members' of the Foreign Ministry opposition to the specialists remaining in Iraq had been expressed, on moral grounds. According to Kondrashov, Defence Ministry staff claimed that the decision must be made by the political leadership, but their Foreign Ministry counterparts argued that the recommendation for withdrawal must come from the military, inasmuch as the personnel belonged to them.[23]

From these comments it could be seen that it was no longer entirely clear just which organs or individuals were vital in the foreign policy decision-making process in a crisis situation. Whereas it was explained that the Party had transferred most of its foreign policy duties to the Foreign Ministry, as the 'ruling party' it aspired to maintain its 'responsibility for the elaboration of the Soviet Union's foreign policy strategy'.[24] According to one military spokesman, neither the military nor the Party was responsible for decisions regarding, for example, arms sales. Lt.-Gen. Nikutich told *Izvestiya* that such decisions, once taken by the Politburo and the Council of Ministers, were now taken by the President and the Council of Ministers.[25] The Council's deputy chairman, Igor Belousov, claimed that arms sales were decided by a sub-division within the Ministry for Foreign Economic Relations with the 'direct involvement' of the Ministry of Foreign Affairs.[26] While the Council of Ministers did set up an interdepartmental committee during the war, under Belousov, to organize the evacuation of Soviet citizens from Kuwait and Iraq, no information was released on the jurisdiction, authority, level of participants or *modus operandi* of this committee. Indeed some of these details may not have been clear to the participants themselves.

An apparently separate 'crisis group' was established, possibly only when the war actually began. Its members consisted of the Defence, Interior, and Foreign Affairs Ministers as well as the head of the KGB, presidential foreign policy aide Chernaev, and presidential adviser Primakov, with the participation also of presidential press aide Ignatenko and Deputy Foreign Minister Belonogov.[27] According to one account, Gorbachev consulted with Vice-President Yanayev, Bessmertnykh, Kryuchkov, Yazov, Primakov, Central Committee International Department chief Falin and 'others' when he was informed of the imminence of the war on 17 January, but only Primakov, Belonogov, Chernaev and Ignatenko were reported to have participated in the critical February talks with Aziz in Moscow.[28] Primakov created his own informal committee of consultants, comprising virtually all the major Middle East experts and some others, to advise him during the crisis.[29]

Almost no mention was made of the Presidential Council's role in the crisis before it was being disbanded at the end of the year. One report in September (gleaned, it was commented, only from 'a great many phone calls') explained that the Council was still in the process of formation, the implication being that it would be 'another few months' before it assumed its function as a 'national security council' modelled on the one in Washington.[30] In any case, according to an interview with Aleksandr Yakovlev (probably conducted before the Gulf crisis), he and the Council were to have only a consultative capacity, interpreting events and advising the President, with no decision-making powers.[31] An interview with Valentin Falin was marginally more explicit. He explained that operational matters were now in the hands of the Foreign Ministry (as distinct from in the past when the Party Politburo 'had to approve virtually every verbal note'), whereas problems of 'a broad state level' were the domain of the Presidential Council. He implied that the Party's role was to express the public mood on those matters 'extending beyond the framework of interstate relations'. While this was not entirely comprehensible, Falin did explain that all three bodies would provide their own, presumably different, analyses and proposals to the President.[32] In November, however, came the surprising announcement that the Presidential Council was to be disbanded. It was eventually replaced by a new National Security Council, to which Primakov was elected (as one of only two persons who were not ministers) to deal specifically with foreign economic matters.[33] The functions, authority and jurisdiction of this Council, however, were no clearer than those of its predecessor.

Equally confusing and potentially even more significant, if not actually explosive, was the difference that appeared between the Supreme Soviet of the Soviet Union and that of the Russian Republic. In September, shortly after the first debate in the International Affairs Committee of the Soviet parliament, the analogous committee of the Russian Republic, chaired by Vladimir Lukin, also debated Soviet policy in the Gulf. Unlike the Soviet parliament, however, the Committee of the RSFSR parliament did not fully approve the government's policy but, rather, demanded the recall of all Soviet specialists in Iraq including the military experts, abrogation of the Soviet–Iraqi treaty, and cessation of the training of Iraqi military personnel in the Soviet Union.[34] The central Soviet media avoided all mention of these decisions or even the fact of the Committee's debate, undoubtedly hoping to avoid the potentially explosive implications of serious criticism of the foreign policy of the Soviet Union by any of its republics.[35] Yeltsin himself refrained from any public disagreement with the central government's Gulf policy, but the appointment of such experienced foreign policy new thinkers as Lukin, to chair the Committee, and Andrei Kozyrev, as RSFSR Foreign Minister, suggested that the question of jurisdiction and decision-making even for foreign policy might add yet a further problem to those facing the increasingly unviable Soviet federal system.[36]

Lessons and ramifications

The domestic debate over the Gulf crisis continued well into the postwar period, the proponents of each point of view drawing appropriately different conclusions regarding the outcome of the war. This too was evidence of the pre-eminence of domestic influences on attitudes towards the crisis. Those who favoured a return to pre-Gorbachev policies, that is a cold-war rather than a new-thinking approach, saw in the crisis the victory of American military hawks advocating a unipolar, US-dominated world, in which Washington determined who and what constituted aggression, and in which military might ruled supreme. For the military among these 'old thinkers' the Iraqi defeat was either the result simply of backward (Iraqi) forces using good (Soviet) arms or not fighting at all, or else the demonstration of a 'technology gap' which necessitated increased investment and development of the Soviet arms industry.[37] Thus for some conservative forces the results of the war fortified their arguments for a strong Soviet military to combat the growing dominance of the United States, along with the need for greater arms production not only for Soviet uses but also for sales and assistance to Third World nations. The Soviet Union would then regain its status as a superpower.[38]

Somewhat more objectively, it was admitted that a technology gap had indeed been revealed by the war, in which Soviet air defence systems had not been a match for the US Tomahawk and HARM missiles.[39] Furthermore, the priority of air strikes over a ground war called into question the role of tanks in future wars (and by implication the lucrative sale of Soviet tanks).[40] It was pointed out by a Western observer, however, that Third World countries did not buy weapons to fight the United States but to fight one another or to hold down their own populations, for which purposes T–72 tanks, for example, were perfectly adequate, as had been demonstrated by Soviet moves in the Baltic republics.[41]

Pro-perestroika forces, however, presented another interpretation, concluding that the crisis had produced an unprecedented display of international cooperation on the basis of universal principles of law, reason and democracy in opposition to aggression and tyranny. Their emphasis was on America's willingness to subordinate itself to the decisions of the United Nations, even with regard to cessation of the hostilities. And to counter nationalists among these forces, or at least the disappointment over the decline in Soviet status, it was possible to argue that it was Soviet pressure for peaceful resolution of the conflict that had stopped the Americans from pushing on to Baghdad. The deputy head of the CPSU's International Department, Andrei Grachev, maintained that 'it was the political impetus from the Soviet side that stopped the Americans short of Baghdad, for it reminded them that other members of the coalition would not follow them'.[42] His was a middle position, which played down the risks to relations between the Soviet Union and the United States and welcomed the existence of differences, rather than total identity, between their respective national interests, as demonstrated in the crisis.

The determination of the Soviet national interest, however, remained elusive. Each component of the domestic debate provided its own definition and then judged Soviet policy in the Gulf accordingly.[43] Having steered his usual zigzag course through even this international crisis, in much the same way as he conducted domestic policy (and for most of the same reasons), Gorbachev may have failed to satisfy any one group and alienated most. One camp contended that Moscow had not done enough to demonstrate its adherence to the new world order and the anti-Iraq coalition, and another complained that Moscow had done too little to attest to its independence as a great power. This dichotomy was, however, symptomatic of the far more significant and pressing differences emerging over perestroika itself and over the way in which the country's overwhelming domestic problems should be overcome.

Thus it was the domestic environment that not only dominated but to a large degree determined Gorbachev's ability to pursue new thinking in foreign policy. Having sought to placate the conservative forces during the winter, Gorbachev turned to the democratic forces in the spring, greatly enhancing his strength by reaching an agreement with Yeltsin in April, followed immediately by the 'nine-plus-one' accord designed to hold the republics of the Soviet federation together. This by no means eliminated the pressures on the Soviet leader, particularly from the right (Party conservatives, the military and so forth) but, fortified by his cooperation with Yeltsin and the democrats (whose popularity was singularly demonstrated in the June elections in Russia), Gorbachev was able to steer a course appropriate to new thinking.

Even as the Gulf war was ending, Gorbachev was apparently aware of the damage his inconsistencies might have caused in Washington (in addition to problems arising with regard to both the conventional weapons accord in Europe and the START talks). He therefore issued a warning about the 'fragility' of the Soviet–American relationship, presumably intended to curb his conservative, especially military, opponents.[44] Theoretically the military, too, should have been concerned about maintaining the relationship with the United States and Western Europe, in view of the need for economic assistance, which would also, of course, benefit the Soviet military machine. Yet the military press, along with *Sovetskaya Rossiya* and other conservative organs, continued to publish strong anti-American diatribes.[45]

But with or without the military's compliance, Gorbachev was able to maintain his positive relationship with the West, to a large degree thanks to American willingness to overlook the temporary Soviet lapses. The last-minute effort by the Soviet Union to prevent the ground war did evoke cries of 'cold war' from certain circles in Washington, fortifying sceptics, probably in the US military, who viewed a number of the winter's lapses by the Soviets as evidence of their continued hostility. The US administration, however, like Gorbachev, chose to draw a different conclusion from Soviet behaviour in the war, focusing rather on the essential role played by Moscow's cooperation with the United States and the anti-Iraq coalition, particularly at the United Nations. Thus, as the properestroika forces in the Soviet Union claimed, Soviet behaviour in the crisis did indeed create a precedent for open and direct Soviet–American cooperation, even collaboration in time of international conflict.

The Gulf crisis, however, also underlined the need to eliminate regional instability if the post-cold-war world order were to be preserved. It demonstrated that regional conflicts not only produced arms races and technological developments which threatened the arms accords reached at the superpower level, but also carried the potential for sudden shifts in regional balances of power that threatened the national interests of one superpower or the other, thereby bringing to the fore potential conflicts in these national interests and creating obstacles to superpower cooperation. The regional challenge to US national interests had elicited a virtually unilateral American action which, as we have seen, for many in Moscow constituted a deviation from the multilateralism that was supposed to replace bipolar competition in the post-cold-war order. This in turn highlighted the asymmetry in Soviet–American relations, in which

Soviet weakness contrasted starkly with American strength, and super-power cooperation appeared to take the form merely of Soviet acquiescence in American policies. In this sense, the regional crisis may simply have revealed (rather than created) the true nature of the superpower relationship. In so doing, however, it produced a challenge to this relationship and threatened to impede future progress. Resolution of regional conflict, therefore, assumed added importance for the Soviet Union.

At the regional level, the crisis had a mixed impact on Soviet relations with the Middle East states and peoples. Support for the anti-Iraq coalition brought Moscow dividends in the form of improved relations with Egypt (with whom relations had already been improving) and, far more significantly, the opening of diplomatic relations with Saudi Arabia. This had been sought for some time by Moscow and expected after the withdrawal from Afghanistan, and was finally accorded by Riyadh as a token of appreciation for Soviet cooperation in the crisis. The Saudi move brought a boost to Moscow's standing in the Gulf region itself, including the opening of relations with Bahrain, and a $4 billion credit from the Kuwaiti government, Saudi Arabia and the United Arab Emirates.[46] Political gains were also registered in Soviet–Iranian relations, as Moscow engaged Tehran in its peace-making trips back and forth to the region. A degree of dissociation from the Americans during the war, as urged by conservatives in Moscow, was of particular importance for the benefits which accrued to the Soviet Union in its dealings with Iran. Following the war, Moscow negotiated a deal to sell Soviet aircraft to Iran, apparently in addition to previously agreed arms deals. On the whole, the warming of Soviet relations with Iran and with the other Gulf states was perceived in Moscow as a major achievement, with a good deal of potential for the sagging Soviet economy.

The Soviet military, however, was concerned over the possibility of an expanded, permanent American military presence in the Gulf as a result of the war. This, along with American arms sales to various Middle East states, was the focus of many of their anti-American diatribes following the war. Acknowledgment of these concerns was apparent in Moscow's proposals in March for postwar arrangements. These called for a reduction of the foreign military presence in the area to the pre-crisis levels, with security to be ensured by the regional actors themselves and the UN;[47] they further suggested the creation of a UN naval force as part of a regional security system. This had originally been proposed by the Soviet Union in the Iran–Iraq war, primarily to remove the expanded US naval presence at that time. Such a system would convert the Gulf into a zone free of weapons of mass destruction; it would be accompanied by balanced cuts in supplies of weapons to the region, beginning with offensive weapons and especially missiles.

How this could be reconciled with Soviet arms sales to the Gulf states was not explained, except by comments in the military press which indirectly justified such deals by reference to new American arms sales to the region. Officially, Moscow was willing to limit such supplies to conventional, defensive weapons only, based on the principle of 'reasonable defensive sufficiency'.[48] This restriction was unlikely to be unilateral, however. In the event of international agreement to such arms controls, Soviet compliance would most probably be dependent, like so many other features of new thinking, on the relative power of conservatives and new thinkers, the former being reinforced by economic considerations on this particular issue. For this reason, there seemed to be a greater likelihood of progress in the area of non-conventional weapons supplies and technology transfer, including missiles, inasmuch as Soviet missile sales fell within the range permitted, for example, by the missile technology control regime (MTCR) accords with which Moscow had agreed to comply as of February 1990.

While Soviet relations with Iran and with the Arab states of the anti-Iraqi coalition improved as a result of the Gulf crisis, Moscow's prestige in the region was not significantly enhanced. Although the Arab coalition states undoubtedly appreciated the Soviet cooperation which facilitated (some might say even enabled) the formation and functioning of the coalition, they were also aware of the clearly subordinate role and importance of the Soviet Union as a power able or willing to act on their behalf. The lessons already being learned prior to the crisis, with regard to the reduced value of Soviet support in view of Moscow's new policies and problems, were now more clearly driven home. While these states appeared to follow the American lead in overlooking the Gorbachev–Primakov lapses, the potentially problematic moves by Primakov, for example, did not have the desired effect on Iraq and the Arab states supporting it. It is possible that there was some gratitude to Moscow for trying to prevent or limit hostilities, but there were reportedly also those in Iraq and elsewhere who dismissed these efforts as merely futile gestures designed to cover up or compensate for what was in fact Soviet cooperation with the anti-Iraq coalition. At the very least, the failure of Primakov's efforts further demonstrated to these elements, as well as to those opposing Iraq, the relative unimportance and ineffectiveness of the Soviet Union in its present situation.

Where the Soviet Union did benefit significantly from its Gulf policy was in the Arab–Israeli conflict, for the United States finally granted Moscow a role in the peace process. This had been promised both by President Bush at the September summit and by Baker in his talks with Bessmertnykh in January 1991, in what was almost openly acknowledged as a quid pro quo for Soviet support in the crisis.[49] The United States did indeed fulfil this commitment, maintaining contact with Moscow during Baker's subsequent peace efforts in the region and according Bessmertnykh a role, primarily vis-à-vis the Soviet Union's own clients, Syria and the PLO, during the Soviet foreign minister's trip there. The Soviet Union was openly declared co-partner with the United States in the plans for a regional peace conference, and neither country denied this cooperation in any way.

Thus, despite the conservative demands for an 'independent' Soviet line, Moscow in fact agreed, as we have seen above, to virtually all of America's tactics and strategies regarding a settlement: the step-by-step approach or interim agreement idea; two-track diplomacy through bilateral talks between Israel and its adversaries, to begin after an opening multilateral session chaired by the Soviet Union and the United States; and apparently also assistance in gaining Syrian and possibly even PLO agreement to these moves as well as to a Palestinian–Jordanian delegation (without East Jerusalemites).

Indeed, if any change occurred in Soviet policy towards the conflict following the Gulf crisis, it was in the direction of still closer cooperation with Washington, further improvement of relations with Israel and a still more muted attitude towards the PLO. In the spring and summer, increasing Soviet support was raised for Palestinian representatives other than the official PLO in Tunis. The Soviet Consul-General in Israel said that cooperation with Palestinians from the occupied territories had begun, while *Izvestiya*'s Middle East editor Skosyrev actually challenged the PLO's right to represent the Palestinians in the absence of elections.[50]

Others questioned Arafat's legitimacy as a leader after his mistaken policy regarding Saddam.[51] Israel, by contrast, gained somewhat in popularity as a result of its restraint during the Iraqi SCUD attacks, and relations between the two countries expanded rapidly from the top government levels down to individual republic accords with Israel. There was even a report of Soviet–Israeli, even Azerbaijani–Israeli cooperation in the field of nuclear energy and a plan to send an Israeli into space aboard a Soviet spaceship.[52]

Shevardnadze's earlier proposals for security arrangements appeared to have been merged with ideas for international limitations on arms supplies (as proposed by the Soviets and the Americans) and disarmament in the realm of non-conventional weapons. While the Soviets spoke of extending a Gulf security structure to include the entire region, they left the initiative on arms issues to the Americans as well. Having already themselves proposed (in Shevardnadze's letter to the UN of 14 August 1991) controls on arms and technology transfers as well as a ban on weapons of mass destruction in the region, they responded positively to the Bush proposals of May 1991 and at the meeting of major arms-supplying states in Paris in July.

The continuity which gradually emerged in Gorbachev's Middle East policy, despite two different foreign ministers and changing senior officials dealing with the region, seemed to provide a reliable indication of future policy. The overriding principles were the priority of cooperative relations with the West, in particular the United States, and the related imperative of regional stability. These did not rule out interests in trade and good relations with the states within the region, but such interests appeared to take second place to the interest in superpower cooperation and stability.

The single most important factor to affect Soviet policy, however, would be the domestic situation. This involved many unknowns, such as the potential influence of Soviet Muslims; the complex relationship between the democratic forces behind Yeltsin and Russian nationalists; the independent actions of various republics and their decision-making bodies; differences within the Soviet Foreign Ministry itself, not only between Arabists and those more neutral but also between those advocating a regional approach and those focusing exclusively on an Arab–Israeli settlement; and differences even within the military, in which conservatives did not speak for all, even at the highest levels. Any or all of these factors could have an impact on Soviet Middle East policy. The Soviet economic situation would also guide certain aspects of this policy, as the Soviets sought profitable trade and commercial relations, especially in the area of energy. Domestic economic distress, however, was likely to to mean that priority would continue to be accorded to the relationship with the West.

The most important variable on the domestic front was, of course, the continuation of perestroika, new thinking and democratization. Just as in the winter of 1990–1 there were (admittedly temporary) setbacks that affected some aspects of Middle East policy, so too future zigzags by Gorbachev, or still more serious domestic challenges to his path, had the potential drastically to change the Soviet view of the West, Soviet defence interests and, therefore, Soviet policies in the region. As perestroika progressed, such drastic change appeared less likely, or less possible. Change in the other direction – that is, Gorbachev's replacement by democratic forces – promised merely to strengthen and accelerate the tendencies that were already propelling Moscow's new policies in the Middle East. And the most striking characteristic of these policies was the Soviet Union's attempt to redefine its role as that of a virtually neutral great power, acting in concert with the United States and the Western democracies to achieve some stability in the region.

6

EPILOGUE: AFTER THE SOVIET UNION

The effects of the coup

The abortive coup of 19–21 August 1991 precipitated a virtual revolution, with incalculable results for the Soviet Union. In so far as future policies with regard to the Middle East were affected, at least three factors stood out:

(1) the defeat of the conservatives, particularly in Russia, and the accompanying demise of the Communist Party, apparat and nomenklatura, the dissolution of the KGB, and the massive restructuring and personnel changes in the military and interior ministry forces which paralleled personnel changes throughout the system;

(2) the strengthening of Russian nationalism as a dominant force, accompanying the near-eclipse of Gorbachev by the hero of the anti-coup resistance, Boris Yeltsin, and the emergence of Russia (and Yeltsin) as coequal with the central organs of power in authority and strength; and

(3) the break-up of the Union following the declarations of independence by nearly all fifteen republics, the dissolution of the Congress of People's Deputies and reconstitution of the Supreme

Soviet (to comprise 20 representatives of each former Union republic plus representatives of the 16 autonomous republics as part of the Union republics' delegations). This was followed by the attempt to forge a new system, based on political, economic, military and scientific accords, to which the republics (or states) might or might not adhere, in whatever form they chose. It was apparently intended to create all-Union bodies which would be subject to strong control and direction by the member republics.

The defeat of the conservatives cleared the way for full implementation of new thinking in all its aspects with regard to the Middle East as well as other areas. Theoretically this meant the unfettered pursuit of cooperation with the West, particularly the United States, with an overriding interest in obtaining economic aid and establishing economic ties, along with a willingness to introduce the kinds of economic and military reforms (including massive cuts in defence spending) demanded by the West. The first concrete signs of this cooperative approach were the agreements for a ban on Soviet and American arms supplies to Afghanistan and for the withdrawal of Soviet forces from Cuba.

Personnel changes were expected to reflect this opportunity fully to implement the cooperative approach, and indeed important architects of this approach, such as Shevardnadze and Yakovlev, found their way back into Gorbachev's advisory bodies, their public authority enhanced by their active role in the resistance to the coup. In November 1991 Shevardnadze actually returned to his former post of Soviet Foreign Minister, although by that time it was unclear just how much authority any central office would be able to exercise. In the interim, following the coup, Bessmertnykh had been replaced by Boris Pankin, a move that promised the continuing implementation of the policies decided at higher levels. Pankin was as much a supporter of new thinking as his predecessor but no more an authoritative figure in his own right than Bessmertnykh. Indeed Pankin had far less experience or knowledge of Middle Eastern affairs, and this suggested that he might rely more on the Ministry's professionals, including Arabists, with regard to Middle East policy. Nonetheless, personnel changes were expected to weed conservatives out of the Foreign Ministry, as well as the Defence Ministry. The appointment of Evgeny Primakov to head the new Foreign Intelligence Agency greatly enhanced Primakov's influence and probably meant that the Middle East would, by virtue of Primakov's own expertise, receive more attention than usual in intelligence, but it was less certain just how dominant a decision-making role the experienced Arabist would be assuming with regard to this region in particular.

The decision regarding Afghanistan promised to serve as a model for relating to the Arab–Israeli conflict or even the region as a whole, that is, cessation of arms supplies at source. But Gorbachev's post-coup policy called for even greater cooperation with the United States than previously, and the United States was pursuing an Arab–Israeli peace conference approach rather than an arms control or regional approach at the time. The only change that might have been expected, therefore, at least with regard to the Arab–Israeli conflict, would have been immediate renewal of full diplomatic relations with Israel, without the conditions set prior to the attempted coup.[1] Yet Moscow was to maintain those conditions; Foreign Minister Pankin announced that relations would be fully renewed only on the eve of the conference. And indeed they were finally renewed only when Pankin and Baker, in Israel, issued the formal invitations to the conference in October 1991, just two weeks before the opening of the conference in Madrid.[2]

The continued, albeit short-lived, reluctance immediately to renew relations with Israel, despite the weakening if not disappearance of the conservative advocates of such a policy, may have reflected Primakov's continued influence, but it may also have been due to the second factor emerging from the August events: the rise of Russian nationalism. It was from this sentiment that Yeltsin's power derived to a large degree, and there were strong Russian nationalists in his entourage. Such people were by no means necessarily anti-Semitic, but some of them clearly were, and some of them were also Arabists by training and profession. These elements, having already opposed the *rapprochement* with Israel and pressed for continued loyalty to the Arabs, may have had some influence on Yeltsin's own positions. The Russian parliament (increasingly important with the break-up of the Union) was known to contain delegates of conflicting views on Middle East issues; discussion about opening Russian diplomatic relations with Israel, for example, had been avoided by the Russian Supreme Soviet's International Affairs Committee in the past because of differences of opinion. To some degree these differences had developed as a result of concern over the interests of or pressures from Muslims inside the Russian Republic, of whom there are close to ten million.

Countervailing pressures, however, may be expected from foreign policy experts such as Russian Foreign Minister Andrei Kozyrev, who has been a staunch advocate of withdrawal from regional conflict, or the still more influential Lukin, who visited Israel in early September. Indeed Lukin and others in the Russian parliament may have been pressing for independent Russian relations with Israel even before the final disappearance of the Union. There may also be those among the Russian nationalists who will support further *rapprochement* with Israel as a rejection of past communist policies and a symbol of new thinking, or out of an interest in the economic benefits to be derived from extensive relations with Israel. In this connection, the presence of hundreds of thousands of their former countrymen in Israel is seen as another factor facilitating economic relations and prompting an interest in good formal ties with Israel. Many Russians, as well as officials of other republics, view Israel not only as a potential partner for commercial relations but as a stepping-stone to ventures with Western companies and Western investment.

Economic motivation, however, also includes the matter of arms sales, for which wealthy Arab states, and Iran, are more promising partners. Yet if such an economic (or any other) interest were permitted to affect political positions dictated by the cooperation with the United States, the broader, more important economic interests vis-à-vis the West might be negatively affected. A key, therefore, to the role of Russian nationalism and the matter of arms sales, as well as to the Muslim factor, will be the relationship of the republics to one another and the degree of coordination within the structure replacing the former Union in the areas of foreign policy and foreign trade.

The Commonwealth of Independent States
The Commonwealth of Independent States which replaced the USSR in December 1991 envisaged its eleven or twelve member states as full and equal members of the international community, with the right to establish

direct diplomatic, consular, trade and other relations with foreign countries, to exchange representatives with them and to conclude international treaties and participate in the activity of international organizations. It was not clear whether any limitations were to be placed on these functions with regard to mutual interests or the interests and commitments of the various member states. For example, some coordination of foreign policy was planned, but it was not certain just how extensive or detailed this was to be, or what mechanism would be employed. Just as a Council of Presidents of the newly independent states was now planned, so too a Council of Foreign Ministers, already created even before the attempted coup, might be formed. In the past this council had been chaired by the Union Foreign Minister, but within the context of the Commonwealth – that is, in the absence of a central authority – the chairmanship would presumably have to be rotated or set up in some way so as to avoid the predominance of one state over another. The role of the foreign affairs committees of the legislatures of each state would also have to be determined in relation to decisions coordinated at the Commonwealth level, along with the relative jurisdiction of and relations between the foreign ministries of each state. To this must be added the other governmental bodies which play a role in foreign relations, namely military, security and economic organs.

Clashes of interpretation if not of actual interests between the various member states, however infrequent, would be bound to occur, particularly as military and economic considerations impinged upon foreign policy decisions. An important problem which had already surfaced revolves around natural resources. Control over its own reserves of oil and natural gas, assumed by Russia after the coup, gave it jurisdiction over the former Union's main export item and source of hard currency. The Russian republic accounts for over 90% of Soviet oil production and 76% of Soviet natural gas. It is difficult to know what effect Russia's intention of tripling the domestic price of its oil and gas will have on the world market. However, the freeing of Russian (or Uzbek or Kazakh) oil production from central Soviet control, permitting the conclusion of individual deals of the type negotiated, for example, by Chevron with the Republic of Kazakhstan, should improve production capacity and change the structure of production and marketing if not prices. A similar result might be expected in other industries, such as fisheries and timber, particularly in Russia. This, as well as competition within and between republics, depending upon the degree to which the market system and privatization are introduced, can be expected to have an effect on foreign business arrangements and possibly in more general terms on the foreign affairs of Russia as well as the other republics.

There may be an effort to subject the military industries to central coordination or even controls but they too, like natural resources, are already being expropriated by the republics in which they are located. The autonomous regions and districts, in Russia for example, are also presumably going to want to share in, if not totally control, the profits from these industries. Even if there is some central coordination, there is likely to be considerable competition between enterprises in different states and between states. This could affect foreign contracts, conditions and prices in the area of military deliveries – with potentially serious foreign policy ramifications.

The military itself promises to be a far less significant arm of foreign policy than previously. It appears that there will be at best a limited joint force for all the states in the Commonwealth, while Ukraine and others have already begun to form their own armies. Thus both the size of the emerging military forces and the ability to deploy them beyond Commonwealth borders will be greatly reduced by the reforms and constitutional changes being introduced. Not only will it be necessary to gain parliamentary approval for the deployment of troops outside, it may also become necessary for even some Commonwealth force or command to negotiate with the local governments in the border areas, for example, in order to station or transport troops through their territory. At the same time, it is at least theoretically possible that states bordering on the Middle East, for example Azerbaijan, might one day seek to use their own forces abroad, independently.

The Muslim factor

The 'Muslim factor' takes on a somewhat different meaning with the break-up of the Soviet Union, for it is possible to conceive of a 'Muslim' foreign policy: that is, a policy by the Muslim republics orientated towards and possibly determined by interests in links with the Muslim countries of the Middle East and Asia. Even before the attempted coup, the five Central Asian republics had joined together in a cooperative, mainly economic, union; their Central Asian identification may well guide them in foreign policy too, as they seek to expand the cultural and economic links already established with Muslim countries. Moreover, as they combat what may be perceived as Russian domination or influence, from the millions of Russians living in the Muslim republics (particularly Kazakhstan) as well as from the centre, their identification with Islam may become stronger. With the exception of Kyrgyzstan, the Muslim republics continue to be ruled by autocratic communists, and the unrest caused by this in the period after the attempted coup saw a rallying of religious as well as democratic forces against these rulers (despite the fact that many of these communists had been espousing nationalism, as they had once espoused communism, as an instrument of power).

Yet as already pointed out, the Muslim factor is an extremely complicated one. Even if the Muslim republics move beyond their preoccupation with domestic issues and internal problems, it is not certain that their foreign policy efforts will be directed any more towards the Arab or Islamic countries than, for example, towards Muslim but secular Turkey, which holds a strong appeal for the mainly Turkic populations of Central Asia and Azerbaijan. With the exception of Tadzhikistan, as we have seen, Islamic fundamentalism may hold little attraction for the many ethnic groups concerned. Indeed the predominance of Sunni Muslims over Shi'ites in Central Asia limits the influence of Iran and its fundamentalism, while the Turkish origin of even some Soviet Shi'ites may have the same effect. Turkey, and even China (with nearly ten million Muslims in neighbouring Sinkiang) may command greater interest because of ethnic ties.

Moreover, economic interests rather than nationalist or religious inclinations have already been dictating many of the contacts between the Muslim republics and the outside world. Such contacts may be expected to include expansion of the already emerging commercial relations with non-Muslim countries such as South Korea, Japan and even Israel. Israel is regarded not only as a stepping-stone to American business but as a potentially useful partner for trade and cooperation in the areas of agricultural goods and technology, high-tech industry and diamonds. Azerbaijan has already concluded some contracts with Israel and discussed cooperation in nuclear research with Israel's (extreme right-wing) Science Minister, Yuval Ne'eman.

The oil-rich but economically backward Kazakhstan may find it more beneficial to deal extensively with countries like Japan and South Korea rather than the spiritually closer but also oil-rich countries of the Middle East. Indeed, unburdened by the political problems between the Soviet Union/Russia and Japan over the Kuriles, republics like Kazakhstan will be free to develop vigorous economic relations with the Japanese, who have already indicated their interest in making Kyrgyzstan a model case for economic relations with their own country. While investment may be preferred from Muslim countries, for example in the banking sphere, these republics and their component parts may well look elsewhere when it comes to seeking technology and manufactured goods. Thus it is not a foregone conclusion that the Muslim republics will necessarily become allies of the Arab states and/or Iran or even play an important, independent role in the region. Complex cultural, social and economic factors, as well as the still undetermined political arrangements, may produce foreign policies of a far more ambiguous nature.

If the Middle East interests of even the Muslim republics remain unclear, those of the newly independent Ukraine and powerful Russian Republic are almost totally unformed. Their orientation and concentration will presumably be westward, towards Europe and the United States, while economic interests will direct some of their efforts towards Asia as well. Natural markets for their goods may be found in the region, but the economic assistance and investment as well as trade needed from Europe and the West in general will probably tie these two states (and the Commonwealth as a whole) more closely to the European than to the Middle Eastern economies. Politically it has already become clear that the interest and role of the former Soviet Union in the Middle East is marginal. Indistinguishable from the United States in its policies, weakened and preoccupied with internal strife, Moscow, even before the break-up of the Union, had virtually ceased to be a player in the Middle East arena in any but a purely symbolic way. The United States has continued to grant Russia a certain status, acknowledging it as successor to the Union and relating to it as if it still constituted a world power. But Russia itself has evinced little interest in the region. The traditional geopolitical interests of those states bordering on the region will presumably remain; ethnic, religious and also economic interests will lead in various directions. Regional stability, however, for the pursuit of both international and domestic interests, may well remain the preferred condition for the new states emerging from the former USSR.

NOTES

The following abbreviations have been used:
FBIS: Foreign Broadcast Information Service (Soviet and Near East – SOV and NES)
JPRS: Joint Publications Research Service

Chapter 2: New thinking in Soviet foreign policy

1 For a discussion of the new military doctrine, see Christoph Bluth, *New Thinking in Soviet Military Policy* (London, RIIA/Pinter, 1990).

2 Party Secretary Vadim Medvedev elaborated on much of this in 'The Great October and the Contemporary World', *Kommunist*, no. 2, January 1988, pp. 3–18; see also Sergei Rogov, 'The Interaction of the USSR and US Interests', *SShA: ekonomika, politika, ideologiya*, no. 8, 1988, pp. 3–13; Georgy Kunadze, 'On the Defensive Sufficiency of the USSR Military Potential', *Mirovaya ekonomika i mezhdunarodnye otnosheniya*, no. 10, 1989, pp. 68–83.

3 See, for example, Andrei Kozyrev, 'Confidence and the Balance of Interests', *International Affairs* (Moscow), no. 11, 1988, p. 8; or Richard Ovinnikov, 'The Main Components of a Stable World', *International Affairs* (Moscow), no. 6, 1988, p. 16.

4 See, for example, Andrei Kolosov, 'Reappraisal of USSR Third World Policy', *International Affairs* (Moscow), no. 4, 1990, pp. 34–42; Rogov,

'Interaction', pp. 3–13.

5 See Rogov, 'Interaction'; Kunadze, 'Defensive Sufficiency'; and Andrei Kolosovsky (Assistant Deputy Foreign Minister and possibly the same person as the above Andrei Kolosov), 'Regional Conflicts and Global Security', *Mirovaya ekonomika i mezhdunarodnye otnosheniya*, no. 6, 1988, pp. 32–41, and 'Risk Zones in the Third World', *International Affairs* (Moscow), no. 8, 1989, pp. 38–49; Kolosov, 'Reappraisal'.

6 Andrei Melville et al., 'Prospects for a New US–Soviet Relationship: Perceptions of the Soviet Foreign Policy Community', Research Paper no. 2, Marjorie Mayrock Centre for Soviet and East European Research, Hebrew University of Jerusalem, Jerusalem, 1989.

7 In an interview in *Izvestiya*, 26 June 1990, Deputy Foreign Minister Vladimir Petrovsky enthusiastically endorsed the idea of a Supreme Soviet discussion of the issue. For the debate which erupted during the Gulf crisis see Galia Golan, 'The Test of "New Thinking": The Soviet Union and the Gulf Crisis', in George Breslauer, Harry Kreisler and Benjamin Ward (eds.), *Beyond the Cold War: Conflict and Cooperation in the Third World* (Berkeley, CA, Institute of International Studies, University of California, 1991).

8 General estimates in the West that arms sales accounted for roughly 20% of Soviet hard-currency earnings appear to have been exaggerated in view of the failure of most clients to pay. Andrei Kolosov, described only as a political analyst, wrote: 'The claim that arms deliveries yield us enormous hard-currency profits seems, at this juncture, nothing more than a myth. Of course, individual transactions are profitable, but they have long been cancelled out by all sorts of debts and gratuitous deliveries.' ('Reappraisal', p. 40.) See also Yury Kornilov, *Literaturnaya gazeta*, 31 January 1990; comments on statistics published in *Izvestiya*, 1 March 1990; or Andrei Kolosovsky, 'Risk Zones', pp. 44–5, and his even earlier 'Regional Conflicts', pp. 32–41; A. V. Kozyrev, *Izvestiya*, 21 February 1990; Georgy Mirsky, *Pravda*, 24 August 1989; A. Kireyev, *Pravda*, 18 April 1989; Petr Litavrin, 'The Issue of Arms Trade Limitation', *SShA: ekonomika, politika, ideologiya*, no. 1, 20 December 1988, pp. 13–20. *Izvestiya*, 22 July 1991, raised the issue once again when Angola's debt was reportedly cancelled, claiming that 'the overwhelming proportion of deliveries were made without particular hopes of payment merely in order to bind the leadership of these [recipient] states more closely to our then military-political course'.

9 Maj.-Gen. G. Kirilenko in *Krasnaya zvezda*, 21 March 1990. According to an article in *Argumenty i fakty*, no. 29, 1989, arms accounted for 31% of

Soviet exports, second only to energy-related products.

10 Speaking of the 90 billion rouble debt owed the Soviet Union, Evgeny Kiselev quoted Admiral Grishin, Deputy Minister for Foreign Economic Relations, to the effect that revelation of the debt owed for arms deliveries would cause 'another outburst of emotion among the public' and 'an information bomb' (Moscow television, '120 Minutes', 7 August 1990). In response to the pressure for information, the chairman of the State Commission for Military-Industrial Affairs said in January 1991 that Soviet military exports for the preceding five-year period had totalled 56.7 billion roubles, of which 9.7 billion roubles' worth were exported in 1990; military assistance accorded without recompense amounted to 8.5 billion roubles (*Pravitel'stvenny vestnik* no. 2, January 1991, p. 12 in JPRS–UMA, 8 July 1991, pp. 1–2).

Chapter 3: The Arab–Israeli conflict

1 Gorbachev called for the linkage of superpower *rapprochement* and resolution of regional conflict in *Pravda*, 2 June 1988 and the Politburo was reported to have approved the application of 'new political thinking' to the Middle East in April 1988 (*Pravda*, 15 April 1988).

2 For Soviet interest in the Arab–Israeli conflict and the declining Soviet role in the region during the Brezhnev years, see Galia Golan, *Soviet Policies in the Middle East from World War II to Gorbachev* (Cambridge, Cambridge University Press, 1990).

3 Shevardnadze referred to this in his speech in Cairo, TASS, 23 February 1989.

4 See John Hannah, *At Arm's Length: Soviet–Syrian Relations in the Gorbachev Era*, The Washington Institute Policy Paper no. 18, Washington DC, 1989.

5 See Soviet mention: USSR Foreign Ministry, 'The Foreign and Diplomatic Activity of the USSR', *International Affairs* (Moscow), no. 1, 1990, p. 93.

6 Term used in an *Izvestiya* answer (18 November 1989) to a reader's complaints about such a lobby.

7 See, for example, his comments in Amman, *Petra–JNA* (Jordan News Agency, Amman), 28 June 1990 and *al-Ra'y*, 29 June 1990 (FBIS–NES–90–126, 29 June 1990, pp. 30–31).

8 See discussion 'The USSR and the Third World', *International Affairs* (Moscow), no. 12, 1988, p. 138. Deputy Foreign Minister Yuly Vorontsov, later named ambassador to the UN, is also rumoured to be opposed to the new position on the conflict but close to Yeltsin.

9 See Naumkin interview in *al-Sharq al-Awsat* (London), 8 July 1990 (FBIS–SOV–90–134, 12 July 1990, pp. 17–18).

10 See, for example, Geivandov (who recently left journalism), *Izvestiya*, 30 March 1988, 18 December 1988 and 9 February 1989; Belyaev on Soviet radio, 4 December 1988 and 5 March 1989 or in 'Middle East Versions', *International Affairs* (Moscow), no. 6, 1988, pp. 55, 63, 79; and Smirnov in *al-Anba* (Kuwait), 27 May 1988, *Izvestiya*, 6 September 1989; *al-Majallah* (London), 20 February 1990 (FBIS–SOV–90–033, 16 February 1990, pp. 24–5).

11 Interfax, 11 June 1991.

12 The complexity of the Muslim factor was apparent, however, from the fact that some Muslim republics, such as Azerbaijan, were seeking commercial relations with Israel as well, even to the point of hosting Israeli Science Minister Yuval Ne'eman in May 1991. For an excellent examination of the complexities of Muslim sentiment in the Soviet Union, see Yaacov Ro'i, 'The Islamic Influence on Nationalism in Soviet Central Asia', *Problems of Communism*, July–August 1990, pp. 49–64.

13 For example, the openly anti-Semitic and anti-Zionist writer E. Evseev (now deceased), in the army daily *Krasnaya zvezda*, 30 January 1990; or the 'Letter of the Writers of Russia' published in *Moskovskii literator* and *Literaturnaya Rossiya*, 2 March 1990, as reported in *The Soviet Union and the Middle East*, Marjorie Mayrock Centre for Soviet and East European Research, vol. XV, no. 3, 1990, pp. 13–14.

14 The military was not a solid, unified bloc with regard to perestroika; there was a group called 'Servicemen for Democracy', headed by officers of the highest ranks. (See, for example, references on Russian television, 28 May 1991, to this group supporting Yeltsin's candidacy for the presidency of the Russian Republic, FBIS–SOV, 21 June 1991, p. 27.)

15 Bovin was named ambassador to Israel when relations were finally renewed in October 1991.

16 Tatiana Karasova, head of the Israel desk in the otherwise conservative Oriental Institute, was also a member of the Committee for Renewed Relations with Israel.

17 Until early 1991 Terasenko was head of Planning and Assessments (and played a large role with regard to the Arab–Israeli peace process). By early 1991 Terasov had been named ambassador to Saudi Arabia and Terasenko had left the Foreign Ministry to join Shevardnadze in the creation of a new foreign policy association.

18 This came in an anti-Semitic tract which accused Yakovlev (by implication mistaken for a Jew) of promoting Jews (specifically, it was

alleged, Primakov and Arbatov) to positions of power, and of pressuring Gorbachev to renew relations with Israel. The demonstration was sponsored by the Union of Soviet National Organizations early in 1990. See *KUNA* (Kuwait News Agency) in English, 18 February 1990 (FBIS–SOV–90–034, 20 February 1990, p. 31).

19 See V. V. Zhurkin and E. M. Primakov, *Mezhdunarodnye konflikty*, (Moscow, Mezhdunarodnye otnosheniya, 1972).

20 Bessmertnykh had been a deputy foreign minister responsible for the Middle East as well as the United States prior to his last position as ambassador to Washington. Thus he was well versed in the region and its problems.

21 In response to provocative questions from an Arab journalist in Moscow, *Jerusalem Post*, 3 June 1990. Yeltsin and the democrats adopted the 'new thinking' approach to the region, but their sometime alliance with Russian nationalists and the presence of such nationalists among Yeltsin collaborators may have had an influence of a different type. Members of the Supreme Soviet of the Russian Republic also suggested that the Russian Republic open diplomatic relations with Israel, although the International Affairs Committee was split on the matter. The Committee did seek relations with its counterpart in the Israeli Knesset, but Jerusalem was reluctant to open direct relations with the republics at that time. The change in Washington's attitude to dealing with the Russian Republic after Yeltsin's election to its presidency did not alter such reluctance in Israel, although visits to various Soviet republics were made by Israeli government ministers, as we shall see below.

22 *Pravda*, 25 April 1987.

23 The early stages were quite restrained on the Soviets' part, refusing reciprocity, for example; Israelis were not allowed to come to the Soviet Union either in a consular mission or any other capacity, while Soviet officials and groups were sent to Israel. By early 1988, however, even this reticence had disappeared.

24 At this time the Deputy Director-General of the Israeli Foreign Ministry, Yeshayahu Anug, said that Israel and the Soviet Union were engaged in '*de facto* normalization without calling it that' (*Jerusalem Post*, 23 February 1989).

25 The Israeli Consul-General Aryeh Levin presented his credentials on 25 December 1990. Announcement of this decision came after Shamir and Shevardnadze held talks in Washington in December 1990, amidst rumours that direct flights would also finally be allowed between the two countries. Such flights actually did commence between Tel Aviv and

Moscow, and later between Tel Aviv and Riga and Baku, but on a 'charter basis' so as to exclude the transporting of emigrants to Israel. Only after restoration of full diplomatic relations was this restriction lifted. Trade, too, began to develop between the two countries, with the Soviet Union interested particularly in Israeli agricultural products, agricultural technology, high-tech and diamond industries.

26 There had been a public debate on the issue of resumed relations, triggered by an article by Aleksandr Bovin in *Izvestiya* on 26 August 1989, strongly advocating renewal of relations. A negative response was written (*Izvestiya*, 22 September 1989) by Aleksandr Zotov, who was actually a new thinker very much associated with the idea of *rapprochement* with Israel. His surprising position may have been prompted by an effort to improve his image in the eyes of Syria where he was serving as ambassador. After a number of negative responses from Arab writers, Bovin published a summary of letters sent to the paper in response to the debate; he said that the letters were 9 to 1 in favour of renewed relations with Israel (*Izvestiya*, 25 January 1990). Shevardnadze, a few months after his resignation, told an interviewer he was 'sorry' he had failed to have full diplomatic relations restored, commenting that 'regrettably we are divided in our country on this score, as the world is' (Interfax, 21 May 1991).

27 A Soviet broadcast to Israel in June 1990 said that the only condition was now the 'internationalization of solutions', instead of the former demand for 'agreement to withdraw from all territories occupied since 1967' (Moscow Radio Peace and Progress in Hebrew, 5 June 1990; FBIS–SOV–90–109, 6 June 1990, p. 45). It explained that this did not even mean 'the achievement of concrete results with regard to the solution of the Middle East problems, but rather only the beginning of a political process'.

28 For example, *Sovetskaya Rossiya*, *Leningradskaya pravda* or *Moskovskaya pravda*. Another source of anti-Israel reporting has been *Krasnaya zvezda*, which has published comments by TASS's consistently anti-Israel political commentator Aleksandr Balebanov, as well as the former chairman of the Committee Against Resumption of Diplomatic Relations with Israel, Evseev (see note 13 above). See Stefani Hoffman, 'Shades of Gray: The Current Soviet Press on Israel and Zionism', Marjorie Mayrock Centre for Soviet and East European Research, Research Paper no. 70, Hebrew University of Jerusalem, June 1989.

29 Sergei Rogov and Vladimir Nosenko, 'What "A" Said, What "B" Said', *Sovetskaya kultura*, 9 February 1989. See also comments by the Soviet Minister to Britain, Aleksandr Golitsyn, delivering a speech instead of

then Middle East Department deputy head Terasov, quoted in *Davar*, 23 November 1989.

30 Rogov and Nosenko, 'What "A" Said, What "B" Said', and interview with Nosenko in *Argumenty i fakty*, no. 49, 3–9 December 1988. See also Aleksandr Bovin in *Izvestiya*, 25 January 1990, and a new definition of Zionism as the 'way of thinking and operating, directed at repatriation to Israel, the historic homeland of their [the Jews'] ancestors' (Lev Aleinik, *Izvestiya*, 27 May 1991). Aleinik, in an article reporting on the Zionist conference in Moscow, went on to explain that 'only recently the Zionist movement was ruthlessly persecuted in the USSR. Thousands of destinies were destroyed because of a desire to carry out their right, written in the International Declaration of Human Rights, the freedom to choose their place of residence.'

31 The Foreign Ministry was not willing to propose abrogation of the 1975 UN resolution declaring that 'Zionism is racism', but officials said that Moscow would not oppose such a proposal if it came from the United States and other countries. In November 1991 the Soviet Union cooperated with the United States in bringing about the rescinding of the resolution in the UN General Assembly.

32 *Pravda*, 22 July 1990. At the same time the Soviets began to permit Soviet Jews to visit relatives in Israel for up to three months as early as 1988, when travel between the two countries was still an unusual phenomenon.

33 The restrictions laid down originally by the Jackson–Vanik amendment were suspended for six months on 2 December 1990 and for an additional year on 2 June 1991. Between January 1990 and October 1991 some 320,000 Soviet Jews had emigrated to Israel.

34 Interestingly, the Soviets too maintained this distinction; there was virtually no correlation between waves of official anti-Semitism in the Soviet Union in the 1970s, for example, and Moscow's positions on the Arab–Israeli dispute. (See Jonathan Frankel, 'The Anti-Zionist Press Campaigns in the USSR 1969–1971: An Internal Dialogue', and 'The Soviet Regime and Anti-Zionism: An Analysis', Research Papers nos. 2 and 55, Marjorie Mayrock Centre for Soviet and East European Research, Hebrew University of Jerusalem, Jerusalem.) In the absence of Soviet–Israeli relations, and to the benefit of Israel, emigration became the subject of Soviet–American relations, with the United States dictating its own set of linkages (the Jackson–Vanik and Stevenson amendments), in view of the Americans' advantageous position vis-à-vis the Soviet need for detente at the time.

35 Joseph Heller, *LEHI*, Mercaz Shazar-Keter Publishers, Jerusalem, 1989 (in

Hebrew).

36 *Jerusalem Post*, 8 June 1987, 24 October 1987, 13 and 23 January 1989; *New York Times*, 21 November 1987. Whereas Shamir had initially said (*Ma'ariv*, 3 October 1986, for example) that he opposed such a conference because of the constellation of states that would be opposing Israel there, including the Soviet Union, he subsequently, in the above interviews, said that his opposition to a conference was based on the subjects that would be discussed there, that is, territorial compromise, or on his preference for direct negotiations.

37 *Jerusalem Post*, 8 September 1989.

38 The statement, according to the *Jerusalem Post* was: 'Big immigration requires Israel be big as well'. The paper continued (incorrectly): 'The flood of immigrants made it imperative that Israel maintain its hold on the territories, he said, as "we need the space to house all the people"' (*Jerusalem Post*, 15 January 1990).

39 During his trip to Washington in January 1990, Yitzhak Rabin, too, spoke of what he called the failure of glasnost to reach the Middle East in his effort to bolster US military support for Israel.

40 Similar moderating pressures even in the pre-Gorbachev period had always been at least officially ignored or dismissed out of hand by Israeli governments.

41 Radio Damascus, 27 March 1989 (FBIS–NES, 28 March 1989).

42 The number of Soviet military advisers in Syria was also reduced, although this may merely have indicated the termination of the temporary assignment of large numbers of advisers to train the Syrians on the new weapons provided by Moscow after the Lebanon war.

43 TASS, 29 December 1989.

44 *Al-Qabas*, 25 October 1989; *The Financial Times*, 20 November 1989. It was also rumoured earlier, in the spring of 1988, that Moscow had turned down a proposal from Damascus for a visit by Assad (*New York Times*, 1 May 1988).

45 Radio Monte Carlo, 1 May 1989 (JPRS–TAC, 16 May 1990, p. 23); *Jane's Defence Weekly*, 9 December 1989, p. 1264.

46 Press conference in Moscow, Reuters, 18 September 1989; interviews to *Washington Post* and *The Financial Times*, *International Herald Tribune*, 21 November 1990.

47 *Washington Post*, 20 November 1989.

48 *The Financial Times*, 20 November 1989.

49 *Pravda*, 25 April 1987.

50 TASS, 23 February 1989.

51 *The Financial Times*, 28 March 1989.

52 *New York Times*, 9 March 1990; Radio Damascus, 16 December 1988 (FBIS–NES, 29 December 1988) which said: 'What is called the balance of interests cannot be achieved in the Middle East, where the nature of the problem and the conflict differs from other regional problems and conflicts. Anyone remote from the region and taken in by the brilliance of the detente process can be dragged into the position of equating the aggressor with the victim of aggression, the occupier and the one whose land is occupied, the colonialist with the settler and the one who is stripped of his land and expelled from his home and country. The Arabs can be subjected to various forms of pressure to take part in a hasty operation for a regional settlement ... Thus an alert and dynamic Arab stand is required, capable of dealing with the new international and regional situation.'

53 TASS, 19 February 1989.

54 Journalist and Middle East specialist Andrei Ostal'sky suggested this in *Izvestiya*, 8 March 1990.

55 The minor concession was to refrain (until late 1991) from implementing the agreement on direct Soviet–Israeli flights; hence the fiction of conducting such flights on a charter basis so as to exclude emigrants.

56 There were rumours that the Syrians were particularly put out by the fact that this *rapprochement* was marked by a visit to Moscow by Egyptian Foreign Minister Maquid just at the time when a bid for a visit by Assad had been rejected in Moscow (*New York Times*, 1 May 1988).

57 TASS, 11 May 1989.

58 *Pravda*, 6 July 1989.

59 *Al-Qabas*, 29 August 1989 (FBIS–NES, 31 August 1989).

60 *Izvestiya*, 25 September 1989.

61 *Pravda*, 17 October 1990.

62 From February to July 1991 there were repeated reports that a deal had been struck. The figure ranged between $2 billion and $8 billion, but the lower figure was most frequently cited. This was said to include the latest Soviet tanks, aircraft and air-defence systems, without indicating if the overall figure were for one year (a reversion to pre-1985 high levels – $2 billion a year on average) or for a five-year period as was customary (which would be a severe reduction on even the 1985–9 yearly average of $1 billion). With regard to the Czechoslovak-made tanks, President Vaclav Havel decided in the summer of 1991 to cancel the deal with Syria, at least in part.

63 See Galia Golan, *The Soviet Union and the Palestine Liberation*

Organization: An Uneasy Alliance (New York, Praeger, 1980) or 'The
Soviet Union and the PLO', in George Breslauer (ed.), *Soviet Strategy in
the Middle East* (Boston; London, Unwin Hyman, 1990). For comparison
with Soviet treatment of other national liberation movements, see Galia
Golan, *The Soviet Union and National Liberation Movements in the Third
World* (London, Unwin Hyman, 1988).

64 The Soviets had long pressed for communist acceptance on the executive
but the PLO had refused over the years, primarily in the interests of
maintaining its independence. For Soviet efforts to gain influence within
the organization, see Golan, *The Soviet Union and the Palestine Liberation
Organization*. See also Galia Golan, 'The Soviet Union and the Palestinian
Issue', in Breslauer (ed.), op. cit., pp. 61–98.

65 *Pravda*, 10 September 1988; 12 October 1988; interviews with Deputy
Foreign Minister Petrovsky (*al-Hawadess*, London, 21 October 1988), and
with Foreign Ministry Middle East Director Polyakov (*Le Quotidien de
Paris*, 13 October 1988); Moscow domestic radio, 23 October 1988
(FBIS–SOV, 25 October 1988).

66 *Al-Ittihad* (Abu Dhabi), 18 January 1989, quoted a Soviet Foreign
Ministry official as revealing that 'the intensive consultations conducted
between Moscow and the PLO have helped in formulating the new PLO
stand toward the peace process in the region'. See also Terasov in *al-Anba*
(Kuwait), 7 January 1989, and Abu Mayzen interview with *Izvestiya*, 30
April 1989.

67 See, for example, *Pravda*'s senior commentator Pavel Demchenko, 10
September 1988; Polyakov, *Le Quotidien de Paris*, 13 October 1988; or
Deputy Foreign Minister Petrovsky according to *KUNA* (Kuwait), 14
October 1988, citing *al-Qabas*.

68 The PLO office in Moscow had in fact held diplomatic status since 1981,
so the significance of the 1990 change was not fully clear. It came at the
time of a visit to the USSR by a member of the Israeli government,
Science Minister Ezer Weizman, and therefore may have been intended to
balance this gesture towards Israel. While the Soviets subsequently
referred to the Embassy of Palestine, they did not take the commensurate
step of naming an ambassador to Palestine, although there was a minister
in the Soviet embassy in Tunis, Gromyko's former interpreter Robert
Turgayev, who dealt with the PLO there.

69 Reuters, 7 December 1989, carried US State Department as well as Israeli
embassy praise for Moscow's cooperation on this.

70 For the Soviet attitude towards terrorism and armed struggle, generally and
with regard to the PLO, see Galia Golan, *The Soviet Union and National*

Liberation Movements in the Third World.

71 See Galia Golan, *Gorbachev's 'New Thinking' on Terrorism*, The Washington Papers, Praeger, New York, 1990, for this and the discussion which follows.

72 TASS, 22 June 1990; Amman domestic radio, 7 July 1990, citing an Arab diplomat source in Tunis regarding a letter to Arafat (FBIS–NES, 9 July 1990). There were other Soviet media objections to the US suspension of the dialogue, mainly arguing that Arafat had dissociated himself from the Abul Abbas attempt.

73 Shishlin, Moscow television, 23 March 1991 (FBIS–SOV, 25 March 1991, p. 2); *Izvestiya*, 20 March 1991 (Bovin); *Izvestiya*, 16 May 1991 (Skosyrev).

74 *Kol Israel* (Voice of Israel), 11 June 1991.

75 There had been criticism of the PLO in the past, usually signifying official grievances if not actual differences of opinion within the Soviet leadership. Under glasnost, however, such comments became more frequent, penetrating and comprehensive, as past Soviet support for the PLO was criticized and PLO policies and behaviour – in Lebanon as well as vis-à-vis Israel – were attacked. See, for example, Moscow television, 'International Panorama', 20 November 1988 (FBIS–SOV, 22 November 1988); Vladimir Nosenko, 'Sowing Fear is Not a Way of Building Peace', *New Times*, no. 12, 1989, pp. 9–11; Vladimir Nosenko, 'A Gun or An Olive Branch?', *New Times*, no. 39, 1989, pp. 12–14; Leonid Medvedko, 'A Time to Throw Stones and a Time to Collect Them', *New Times*, no. 36, 1988, p. 16; Dmitry Zgersky, 'Yasser Arafat in Moscow', *New Times*, no. 16, 1988, p. 9.

76 *Al-Ra'y* (Jordan), 1 February 1989.

77 *Al-Ittihad* (Abu Dhabi), 29 January 1989.

78 Leonid Medvedko, 'A Time to Throw Stones', pp. 16–18; *Pravda*, 18 February 1989.

79 *Pravda*, 18 February 1989.

80 *The Times*, 1 May 1989.

81 Moscow domestic radio, 31 August 1990 (Gorbachev in response to a question from a Palestinian journalist); Reuters, 27 September 1990 (Hourani).

82 Letter from the Palestinian embassy to the Soviet radio, Radio Peace and Progress, 26 September 1990 (FBIS–SOV, 27 September 1990); Dmitry Zgersky interview with Nabil Amr, *New Times*, no. 38, 1990, pp. 6–7; Arafat to *Sawt al-Sha'b* (Amman), 2 June 1991 (FBIS–NES, 3 June 1991, p. 4).

83 See note 38.

84 *Al-Dastur* (Jordan), 2 July 1990.

85 At the close of his summit with Bush in June (Moscow television, 3 June 1990; FBIS–SOV–90–108, 5 June 1990, p. 21). Going further than the United States, the Soviet Union called for a UN Security Council resolution 'to appeal to the Israeli government not to permit acts capable of changing the demographic structure of the territories' in violation of the Geneva Convention (*Izvestiya*, 13 February 1990, on a press conference by First Deputy Foreign Minister Yury Vorontsov). Even as they claimed defensively to the Arabs that Soviet laws (not yet passed) forbade interference with the freedom to emigrate, a number of Soviet officials said that the smooth exit of Soviet Jews might in fact be impaired or suspended if Israel did not provide solid assurances regarding their possible settlement in the territories.

86 Israel radio, 10 May 1991.

87 Until 1974 this had merely been the Palestinians' legitimate rights, but as of September 1974 the Soviets supported the demand for a state.

88 For example, in the talks with Peres in Rome in April 1987, or Brutents's interview in Kuwait, *KUNA*, 3 June 1988 (FBIS–SOV–88–108, 6 June 1988, p. 50), or Gorbachev to Arafat, TASS, 9 April 1988. Indeed, a call-sign of 'old thinkers' or opponents of the new policies was usage of the old three-pronged formula which was totally absent from official statements and leadership pronouncements under Gorbachev. See, for example, Yury Griadunov after he presented his credentials as Soviet ambassador to Jordan, *Petra-JNA* (Jordan News Agency, Amman), in Arabic, 28 June 1990 (FBIS–NES–90–126, 29 June 1990, p. 30), or Oriental Institute deputy head and Middle East expert Vitaly Naumkin, *al-Sharq al-Awsat* (London), 8 July 1990 (FBIS–SOV–90–134, 12 July 1990, pp. 17–18).

89 TASS, February 23, 1989; *Izvestiya*, April 29, 1990 (Shevardnadze speeches). For a discussion of Soviet regional security proposals and possible application of a CSCE approach to the Middle East, see Galia Golan, 'Soviet–Russian Proposals for Regional Security in the Middle East', Woodrow Wilson Center, Washington DC, forthcoming.

90 There were also persons in the Soviet foreign policy establishment who saw regional security and other regional issues as topics which might provide some channels for discussion in the absence of a peace conference, in a CSCE–basket-type approach. (See Galia Golan, 'Soviet–Russian Proposals for Regional Security in the Middle East'.)

91 Press conference following the Helsinki summit, *New York Times*,

10 September 1990, and Baker–Bessmertnykh joint communiqué, *International Herald Tribune*, 28 January 1991.

92 There was Palestinian 'restrained rejoicing' (as described to a Soviet journalist by Palestinians in Tunis) over the resignation, but the only discernible change with regard to a settlement was the near-disappearance of references to Shevardnadze's specific security proposals beyond the more standard ideas of curbs on the supply of non-conventional weapons (*Sovetskaya Rossiya*, 26 December 1990).

93 *Verejnost* (Bratislava), 2 May 1991 (FBIS–SOV, 9 May 1991, p. 8).

94 Moscow radio in Arabic, 1 May 1991.

Chapter 4: The Persian Gulf

1 For Soviet relations with the Gulf states prior to Gorbachev, see Galia Golan, *Soviet Policies in the Middle East from World War II to Gorbachev* (Cambridge, Cambridge University Press, 1990).

2 See, for example, Evgeny Primakov, 'Islam and Processes of Social Development in Foreign Countries of the East', *Voprosy filosofii*, no. 8 (1980), pp. 60–71.

3 The gas pipeline was closed after Iran, in 1980, tried to quadruple the price Moscow was paying for the gas.

4 Kuwait had reportedly been rejected by Washington and only subsequently turned to the Soviets, possibly merely to pressure the Americans into agreeing to reflag, which, of course, they did once Moscow had responded to Kuwait's request.

5 As early as the spring of 1985 the Soviets reportedly pressured the Iraqis to refrain from using surface-to-surface missiles against Iran, presumably to prevent escalation of the war. (See Fred Halliday, 'The USSR and the Gulf War: Moscow's Growing Concern', *Middle East Report*, September–October 1987, pp. 10–11.)

6 See David Pollock, 'Moscow and South Yemen', *Problems of Communism*, May–June 1986, p. 47; Fred Halliday, *Revolution and Foreign Policy* (Cambridge, Cambridge University Press, 1990), pp. 209–17. For Soviet policy towards Yemen prior to Gorbachev, see Mark Katz, *Russia and Arabia: Soviet Foreign Policy Toward the Arabian Peninsula* (Baltimore, Johns Hopkins University Press, 1986); Stephen Page, *The Soviet Union and the Yemens* (New York, Praeger, 1985); Norman Cigar, 'South Yemen and the USSR: Prospects for the Relationship', *The Middle East Journal*, vol. 39, no. 4, Autumn 1985, pp. 775–95.

7 Soviet relations with Saudi Arabia were broken off in 1938. A Soviet

journalist recently explained that, according to a British diplomat who had worked in South Yemen, the reason for the break lay in Stalin's execution of the Soviet ambassador to Saudi Arabia, Kerim Khakimov. Khakimov, according to this account, had had good relations with the Saudis and had even attended a mosque from time to time. This fact was conveyed to Stalin by an informer, leading to Khakimov's recall and execution in 1938, and the Saudi king's angry refusal to have any further dealings with Moscow. (Dmitry Zgersky, 'Our Road to Mecca', *New Times*, no. 40, 1990, pp. 8–9.)

8 See Norman Cigar, 'The Soviet Navy in the Persian Gulf: Naval Diplomacy in a Combat Zone', *Naval War College Review*, vol. XLII, no. 2, Spring 1989, pp. 56–88.

9 The Soviet Union did send a strong protest to the Iranian government, but did not retaliate in any way.

10 See, for example, Soviet government statement, *Pravda*, 4 July 1987. Prime Minister Hussein Musavi told an interviewer that the reason for the improvement in relations with Moscow was the fact that 'the Soviet Union opposes the increasing presence of the military forces of the United States and its allies in the Persian Gulf' (Tehran domestic radio, 17 December 1987, in FBIS–NES, 18 December 1987, p. 50).

11 See TASS, 9 March 1988, which denied any role in Iraq's alteration of the SCUDs and, by implication, condemned the act.

12 For example, *Pravda*, 3 June 1988.

13 In these talks the Soviets supported Iran's position against Iraq with regard to the Shatt-al-Arab dispute, advocating a return to the 1975 Iran–Iraq accord.

14 *Middle East Insight*, November/December 1989, p. 18; Dmitry Zgersky, 'Koran versus Pragmatism', *New Times*, no. 22, 1989, pp. 16–17.

15 An article favourable to Rafsanjani as the pragmatic opponent of the conservative Khomeni followers revealed that Rafsanjani, as speaker of the Iranian parliament, had been invited to Moscow (Zgersky, 'Koran versus Pragmatism').

16 Yakov Borovoi and Dmitry Zgersky, 'Entering a New Stage', *New Times*, no. 27, 1989, p. 9 (Rafsanjani press conference).

17 See Anthony Hyman, 'Soviet–Iranian Relations: The End of Rapprochement?', Radio Liberty Report on the USSR, vol. 2, no. 4, January 26, 1990, p. 17. Igor Belyaev provoked a lively debate in the Soviet press when he noted the role of Islamic fundamentalism in the disturbances, reporting talk in both Iran and the USSR of reuniting the Azerbaijanis in an Islamic Republic (*Literaturnaya gazeta*, 24 January

1990 and 7 February 1990).

18 For the Iranian political aspect, see Safa Haeri, 'War of Words Over Azerbaijan', *Middle East International*, 2 February 1990, pp. 10–11.

19 For Iranian interest in these accords, see Shireen Hunter, 'Iran and the Soviets: The Chill is Gone', *Middle East Insight*, January/February 1990, pp. 17–23.

20 *IRNA* (Tehran, Iranian News Agency), 14 June 1991 (FBIS–SOV, 17 June 1991, p. 18).

21 Maria Kielmas, 'The Soviet–Iranian Deal – More Words Than Substance', *Middle East International*, 21 July 1989, pp. 16–17, minimizes the importance of the energy agreements, both for Iran and for the Soviet Union. In an April 1991 election rally a deputy of the Russian Supreme Soviet said that his company was about to sell 'several dozen' tanks to Iran (German News Agency *ADN*, 30 April 1991, citing Ural-Soviety news agency, FBIS–SOV, 1 May 1991, p. 17).

22 *Ibid.*

23 Tehran television, 7 July 1991; *IRNA*, 11 July 1991 (FBIS–SOV, 9 July 1991, pp. 12–13; 12 July 1991, p. 12).

Chapter 5: The Gulf crisis

1 Iraqi oil imported to the Soviet Union was re-exported to Bulgaria, Romania and India; the loss of this trade would amount to the loss of 2 billion roubles' worth of goods for the Soviet market, according to K. F. Katushev, Soviet Minister for Foreign Economic Relations (*Sovetskaya Rossiya*, 26 August 1990). Deputy Foreign Minister Belonogov, denying that Iraq was in debt to the Soviet Union, gave the parliamentary Committee on International Affairs the following breakdown in dollars: a projected loss of over $800 million in 1990, of which $520 million would result from oil not supplied by Iraq for re-export to India, Bulgaria, Romania and other countries, plus $290 million in the form of goods and services not supplied the Soviet Union (TASS, 30 August 1990). To this was to be added $115 million worth of goods and $700 million worth of financial resources from Kuwait. The last referred mainly to the loss of a subsidy promised by Kuwait for the development of oil extraction in Siberia (although subsequently Kuwait, the United Arab Emirates and Saudi Arabia granted Moscow a $4 billion credit, presumably in return for Soviet support of the coalition). Finally, Soviet economists added indirect losses to the Soviet Union as a result of the crisis, such as increased difficulties in obtaining Western credits, increased payments on the foreign

debt, higher prices for foreign equipment, and reduced repayment of Soviet credits from Third World countries. (See A. Kondakov, 'The Third Oil Shock? Economic Consequences of the Iraqi Aggression in Assessments and Predictions by Specialists', *Ekonomika i zhizn'*, no. 38, 1990, p. 20.)

2 *Sovetskaya Rossiya*, 26 August 1990; TASS, August 30, 1990.

3 Shevardnadze in his speech to the United Nations, *International Herald Tribune*, 26 September 1990.

4 Moscow radio in English to Great Britain, 3 September 1990.

5 Moscow domestic radio, 25 August 1990. He expressed the same sentiments again on Moscow radio, 1 September 1990.

6 *Izvestiya*, 26 June 1990, interview with Petrovsky.

7 Maj.-Gen. Vadim Makarevsky, 'The Threat from the South', *New Times*, no. 34, 1990, p. 12.

8 Interview in *New Times*, no. 33, 1990, p. 6.

9 Igor Belyaev, *Literaturnaya gazeta*, 10 October 1990; Alexei Arbatov, *Moskovskie novosti*, 14 October 1990; Galina Sidorova, 'World Closes In', *New Times*, no. 36, 1990, pp. 4–5.

10 Moscow television, 2 October 1990.

11 This claim was made by, among others, the then Warsaw Pact Commander Vladimir Lobov (interview with Andrei Orlov, TASS, 30 August 1990, in FBIS–SOV, 31 August 1990, p. 12; also cited by Moscow domestic radio commentator Georgievich, 'Observers Roundtable', 2 September 1990 in FBIS–SOV, 5 September 1990).

12 Once he was made Vice-President he gave up his position as Party Secretary.

13 While Shevardnadze was in the West saying one thing, Primakov was travelling around the Middle East (including Iraq) apparently saying another. Shevardnadze, according top priority to US–Soviet relations rather than to Iraq or Arab–Soviet relations, reportedly cabled Gorbachev at one point to cease contact with the Iraqi leadership on the grounds that Primakov might give the Iraqi leader the impression that the coalition would not hold. His advice was not heeded.

14 *International Herald Tribune*, 28 January 1991.

15 TASS, 4 February 1991.

16 *Pravda*, 4 February 1991.

17 Reuters, 25 January 1991; *Libération* (Paris), 12 February 1991; *Nouvel observateur*, 14 February 1991. In response, Bessmertnykh told French Foreign Minister Dumas that only a few dozen Soviet nationals remained in Iraq (*International Herald Tribune*, 13 February 1991). The Soviets

claimed that all of the 7,830 nationals, including 193 military experts, had been evacuated by 9 January 1991.

18 As one Soviet commentator put it: 'During the early stages of the conflict, observers noted the unprecedented fact that the Soviet Union, instead of opposing the West in the Middle East, showed awareness of the threat to world peace posed by the aggressor ... Presently it turned out, however, that many influential forces in our country (the military-industrial complex, above all) are displeased with such a policy.' (Leonid Vasil'ev, 'What is Saddam Hussein Banking On?', *New Times*, 12–18 February 1991, p. 14.)

19 See, for example, the resolution of the deliberations at the end of August (TASS, 30 August 1990). It cited both the importance of restraining the United States from the use of force (calling for a solution through the UN) and the need to review the advisability of recalling the specialists once their dependents were evacuated from Iraq. It expressed support for the government's position, demanding the 'complete and immediate withdrawal of Iraqi troops from Kuwait, the complete restoration of its sovereignty [sic], national independence, and territorial integrity'; it also condemned Iraq's taking of foreign hostages.

20 *Izvestiya*, 1 September 1990.

21 *Ibid.*, 16 September 1990.

22 *Ibid.*, 5 September 1990.

23 *Ibid.*, 4 September 1990.

24 *Pravda*, 13 August 1990 (interview with Yanayev).

25 *Izvestiya*, 16 August 1990.

26 Interview in *Pravitel'stvenny vestnik*, no. 2, January 1991, p. 12 (JPRS–UMA, 8 July 1991, pp. 1–2). According to *Izvestiya*, the sub-division was the Engineering Main Administration.

27 Primakov, *Pravda*, 2 March 1991.

28 *Sovetskaya Rossiya*, 18 January 1991; *Izvestiya*, 22 February 1991.

29 This group was by no means homogeneous and most likely offered quite contradictory advice. The existence of this group, however, contradicted claims in *Komsomolskaya pravda* (14 February 1991) that Soviet Arabists were not consulted during the crisis. The informal committee consisted of Kiselev, Simoniya, Nosenko of IMEMO, Naumkin and Zvyagelskaya of the Oriental Institute, Shumikhin and Kremenyuk of the USA Institute, and Zhurkin, head of the European Institute.

30 *Izvestiya*, 1 September 1990, following the visit by White House chief of staff John Sununu.

31 Soyuz, no. 34, 1990, p. 4.

32 *Pravda*, 20 August 1990. It was amazing that although this interview took place at the height of the Gulf crisis, no reference was made to the crisis or decision-making at the time.

33 The Supreme Soviet elected the following members to the Security Council on 7 March 1991: Vice-President Yanayev, Prime Minister Pavlov, Foreign Minister Bessmertnykh, KGB chief Kryuchkov, Defence Minister Yazov, Interior Minister Pugo, former Interior Minister Bakatin, and Primakov.

34 *International Herald Tribune*, 13 September 1990 and *Post factum*, September 1990. A few weeks later it was revealed that on 4 September a group of 48 Soviet oil specialists in Iraq had sent a letter to the RSFSR parliament calling for assistance in helping some 300 Soviet specialists seeking to return to Russia (*Argumenty i fakty*, 5 September–29 October 1990, p. 5). A similar letter was handed to the Soviet ambassador in Baghdad by a different group, representing 400 specialists, on 1 October (*Izvestiya*, 5 October 1990). The Russian parliament also passed an Appeal on the inadmissibility of sending troops to participate in the Gulf action; Lukin voted against this resolution both because he did not want to send an incorrect signal to Saddam and because he opposed 'isolationism', which shirked responsibility to international law to rebuff an aggressor. (Interviews with Lukin and Russian Foreign Minister Andrei Kozyrev, 'Force vs. Force', *New Times*, no. 3, 1991, pp. 20–21.)

35 Only very indirect references were made in the central press, for example, *Izvestiya*, 16 September 1990.

36 As noted above, some members of the Russian International Affairs Committee proposed the opening of diplomatic relations between Russia and Israel.

37 For example, Soviet Air Force chief Lt.-Gen. Maliukov, *Krasnaya zvezda*, 14 March 1991. It was also claimed that the Iraqi army had been equipped and trained in part by the West, and the Soviet arms in its possession were old models, outmoded by those of the coalition forces (Maj.-Gen. Kutsenko, first deputy head of the Operational Strategic Research Branch of the General Staff, *Sovetskaya Rossiya*, 2 March 1991). See also remarks by the deputy chief of the same branch, Lt.-Gen. Shtepa, *Trud*, 2 April 1991 and *Krasnaya zvezda*, 8 March 1991. Col.-Gen. Filatov, the conservative editor of *Voenno-istoricheskii zhurnal*, claimed that Iraq had not in fact been defeated, even militarily (Moscow central television, 13 April 1991 in FBIS–SOV, 20 May 1991, pp. 70–1). Yazov chaired a conference on 6 June in the Defence Ministry on the lessons of the war, but no information was published as to just what conclusions were drawn (*Krasnaya zvezda*, 8 June 1991).

38 An article in *Trud* (2 April 1991) by a deputy chief of the Centre for Operational Strategic Research of the Soviet army contained most of these points, but his response to a direct question regarding arms sales to Third World countries was hedged, to suit the new demands of perestroika: he said that US aggressiveness would lead states to request Soviet aid, necessitating a Supreme Soviet decision in each case.

39 Gennady Gerasimov in *Sovetskaya kultura*, no. 10, 8 March 1991, p. 12; Andrei Kortunov, Moscow radio in English, 15 March 1991 (FBIS–SOV, 19 March 1991).

40 Gerasimov, *Sovetskaya kultura*, op. cit.

41 CBS correspondent in Moscow, Jonathan Sanders, Moscow radio in English, 15 March 1991 (FBIS–SOV, 19 March 1991).

42 Andrei Grachev, *New Times*, no. 17, 1991, pp. 20–2.

43 Interesting contributions on this discussion of national interests and Moscow's superpower or great-power status were written, for example, by Gorbachev's chief adviser Aleksandr Yakovlev, *Izvestiya*, 27 April 1991; Aleksandr Golts, *Krasnaya zvezda*, 13 June 1991 and Gorbachev's and Yakovlev's adviser Nikolai Shishlin, in *Pravda*, 22 June 1991.

44 Speech in Minsk, Moscow Central Television, 27 February 1991 (FBIS–SOV, 27 February 1991).

45 See, for example, *Krasnaya zvezda*, 31 May 1991.

46 *Izvestiya*, 24 December 1990.

47 *Ibid.*, 19 March 1991.

48 See Galia Golan, 'Soviet–Russian Proposals for Regional Security in the Middle East', op. cit.

49 In September the promised cooperation in the Arab–Israeli context was presented as a continuation of the cooperation achieved in the Gulf crisis (*Washington Post*, 10 September 1990).

50 *Kol Israel*, 11 June 1991; *Izvestiya*, 27 May 1991.

51 *Izvestiya*, 4 March 1991; *Izvestiya*, 20 March 1991; Moscow television, 23 March 1991 (FBIS–SOV, 25 March 1991, p. 2).

52 Moscow radio world service in English, 12 July 1991 (FBIS–SOV, 17 July 1991, p. 21). At the Paris air show in June 1991, the Soviet Minister of Aviation suggested that Israel purchase Soviet hardware, including the new MIG–31, and there were also reports of such an offer regarding a Soviet anti-missile missile. While it was subsequently denied that this was intended as a concrete offer, it was also said that 'the market is the market and any legal client has a right to acquire there any commodity' on a cash basis (Russian television, 17 June 1991; *Izvestiya*, 19 June 1991; *Komsomolskaya pravda*, 12 July 1991).

Chapter 6: Epilogue

1 Direct flights to include Jewish emigrants were, finally, started in the autumn of 1991, but this was actually agreed to during an exchange of visits by delegations of the Transportation Ministries of the two countries in the days just prior to and following the attempted coup.

2 In December 1991 Aleksandr Bovin presented his credentials as the Soviet, and subsequently Russian, ambassador to Israel. He was presumably chosen because of his strong advocacy of renewed relations with Israel (the absence of which, he had argued in 1989, demonstrated a failure to apply new thinking to the Middle East). Even during his years as a speech-writer for Brezhnev and an adviser to Andropov, Bovin had long demonstrated candour, originality, insight and independence in his writings about the Middle East as well as other foreign policy issues. He may also have been chosen as ambassador so as to demonstrate a clear change from the Foreign Ministry's 'Arabists', who had a reputation for pro-Arab and/or anti-Israeli tendencies.